# Oracy for ALL

## Enhancing learning through talk in real classrooms

**Laura Bisiker**

**Together we unlock every learner's unique potential**

At Hachette Learning (formerly Hodder Education), there's one thing we're certain about. No two students learn the same way. That's why our approach to teaching begins by recognising the needs of individuals first.

Our mission is to allow every learner to fulfil their unique potential by empowering those who teach them. From our expert teaching and learning resources to our digital educational tools that make learning easier and more accessible for all, we provide solutions designed to maximise the impact of learning for every teacher, parent and student.

Aligned to our parent company, Hachette Livre, founded in 1826, we pride ourselves on being a learning solutions provider with a global footprint.

www.hachettelearning.com

Although every effort has been made to ensure that website addresses are correct at time of going to press, Hachette Learning cannot be held responsible for the content of any website mentioned in this book. It is sometimes possible to find a relocated web page by typing in the address of the home page for a website in the URL window of your browser.

Hachette UK's policy is to use papers that are natural, renewable and recyclable products and made from wood grown in well-managed forests and other controlled sources. The logging and manufacturing processes are expected to conform to the environmental regulations of the country of origin.

To order, please visit www.HachetteLearning.com or contact Customer Service at education@hachette.co.uk / +44 (0)1235 827827.

ISBN: 978 1 0360 0605 1

© Laura Bisiker 2026

First published in 2026 by
Hachette Learning (a trading division of Hodder & Stoughton Limited),
An Hachette UK Company
Carmelite House
50 Victoria Embankment
London EC4Y 0DZ

www.HachetteLearning.com

The authorised representative in the EEA is Hachette Ireland, 8 Castlecourt Centre, Dublin 15, D15 XTP3, Ireland (email: info@hbgi.ie)

Impression number    10 9 8 7 6 5 4 3 2 1
Year                          2030 2029 2028 2027 2026

Illustrations by DC Graphic Design Limited, Hextable, Kent.
Typeset in the UK.
Printed in the UK.

A catalogue record for this title is available from the British Library.

MIX
Paper | Supporting responsible forestry
FSC
www.fsc.org
FSC™ C104740

# TABLE OF CONTENTS

# About the author

**Laura Bisiker** is a primary teacher and oracy specialist based in Leicester. She works with schools across the region to develop high-quality classroom talk, supporting teachers to place pupil voice at the heart of everyday learning through purposeful discussion, intentional vocabulary use and a belief that every child's voice matters. She co-leads a number of oracy-focused professional development projects across Leicestershire, delivering CPD to more than 50 schools. Alongside her classroom practice, she has worked closely with initial teacher training programmes and is passionate about helping teachers use talk as a powerful tool for learning.

# Introduction

*I keep hearing this word...what is oracy?*

Let's begin by establishing this so the rest of the book makes sense!

Oracy was a term coined by Andrew Wilkinson (1965), a British researcher and educator, in the 1960s. It was intended to show a connection between literacy and numeracy, and to highlight the importance – and, in turn, education's omission – of the vital oral skills needed for success.

Over time, the term *oracy* was replaced by "speaking and listening." By the 1990s, speaking and listening had its own small corner of the literacy curriculum.

In 2014, the updated National Curriculum was published. The token nod to speaking and listening in this document was – forgive me – **embarrassing**.

Speaking and listening were "rebranded" as *Spoken Language*. This stripped out the social elements of speaking and listening and narrowed expectations. The main changes applied to key stages 1 and 2. At key stages 3 and 4, *Spoken Language* was referenced separately, but the main focus remained on reading and writing.

The 2014 English programmes of study stated:

*"Spoken language underpins the development of reading and writing. The quality and variety of language that pupils hear and speak are vital for developing their vocabulary and grammar and their understanding for reading and writing."*

There was little importance given to the value that speaking and listening skills contribute to pupils' academic and future success. Thankfully, professionals who understood the deeper meaning of oracy continued to champion its place in pedagogy and curriculum.

## Misconceptions

When defining oracy, it is crucial to address some very common misconceptions.

Oracy is **not**:

- Elocution.
- An intervention.
- Only for private school pupils.
- Solely about debating skills.
- Just about delivering presentations.
- Talk for Writing.
- Limited to literacy lessons or the responsibility of literacy leads.
- Just another lesson.
- A new flash-in-the-pan initiative (Wilkinson, 1960s!).

## So, what *is* oracy?

Put simply, oracy is quality first teaching. The term "quality first teaching" was coined in policy documents by the UK's *Department for Children, Schools and Families (DCSF)*. These policies were written in the late 2000s to help teachers meet the emerging diverse needs of all learners in mainstream classroom settings.

When practitioners begin to understand the true nature of oracy, their usual response is along the lines of "Oh, but isn't that just good teaching?" To which the answer is: yes. At its core, oracy is about encouraging all students to learn to talk (in both subject matter and personal development), to learn about talk, and to learn through talk in all areas of their school day.

In 2024, the Oracy Education Committee published the report *We Need To Talk*, in which they defined oracy as "articulating ideas, developing understanding and engaging with others through speaking, listening and communication."

To accompany this definition, they highlighted three essential dimensions.

*"These three dimensions – learning to, learning through, and learning about talk, listening and communication – provide a conceptual framework for understanding the role of oracy in education throughout compulsory schooling. Here we provide a fuller account of these three dimensions, along with indicative examples of where they may be effectively integrated within well-designed subject curricula."*

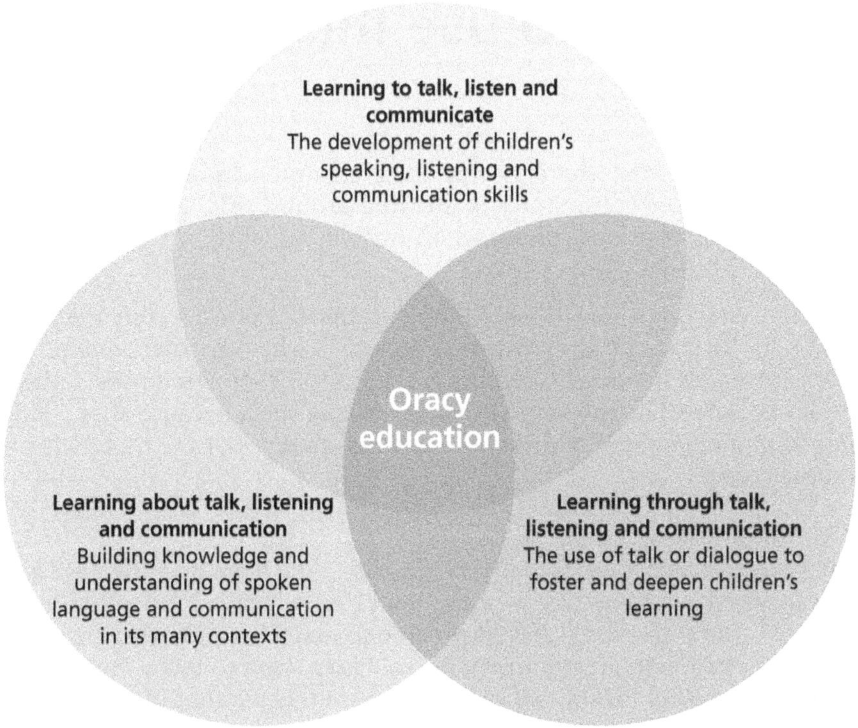

Figure 1 Three dimensions of oracy.

**Learning to talk, listen and communicate**
The development of children's speaking, listening and communication skills

**Learning about talk, listening and communication**
Building knowledge and understanding of spoken language and communication in its many contexts

**Learning through talk, listening and communication**
The use of talk or dialogue to foster and deepen children's learning

Oracy education

## The key to success

The key to success with oracy is cultivating a talk-rich environment where pupils understand what respectful talk looks like and how it is achieved. Pupils should have frequent opportunities to use their voices and practise their listening skills in meaningful ways. For this to happen, all staff must understand *why* oracy matters, what the future aim is for oracy at their school, and what consistent behaviour expectations are that will support this.

This may sound idyllic in outcome but enormous in strategy. It isn't. Hence this book.

Oracy often takes just one lightbulb moment to "click." Once it clicks, the journey is about exploring the strategies available and understanding how they work within schools and individuals' teaching practice.

# How to use this book

I love the fact that there is this buzz around educational research, and that a whole community is growing around this. I'm a big fan of listening to educational podcasts on my way to work – it gets me into the right mindset!

I also love buying a new book. I'll often listen to a podcast, buy the book that gets mentioned and convince myself it will help me become the perfect teacher my overloaded brain aspires to be. However, sadly, these books usually sit on my very scholarly-looking shelf, because after a long day in school I simply don't have the mental capacity or the time to focus on the content.

Does this sound familiar?

My vision for this book is that you can pick it up, open it at any page and feel inspired – almost like a recipe book! As educational professionals, what we want are ideas that improve our practice: ideas that help our students learn more, remember more and help them to make meaningful connections. And ideally, we want to achieve this without increasing our own work or cognitive loads.

Imagine a book equivalent of that course you once went on, the one that made you say "do you know, that was actually really useful! I'm going to go and try that…"

This book is based on conversations with people I've worked with who are passionate about oracy and who have used it successfully within their own practice over a long period of time. Each chapter aims to offer strategies and tips drawn from our shared experiences of embedding oracy within schools, classrooms and wider contexts.

I've been careful to ensure all strategies are manageable and won't detract from our already stretched curriculums and timetables. In fact, when embedded, I hope they will help alleviate some of those pressures.

Please don't put pressure on yourself or your colleagues to embed oracy this term or even this school year. Developing oracy practice takes time. Embedding strategies consistently is a slow process, one that needs passionate leadership and constant banging the drum.

## Cognitive load theory

Within the book I mention cognitive load theory – an absolute game changer for me!

Cognitive load theory is based on the idea that our brains have both working memory space and long-term memory space. The long-term memory space is vast and stores knowledge in organised "schemas" or "mental models", whereas the working memory space is exceedingly limited. The goal of an effective educator is to transfer learning, knowledge and understanding from working memory into long-term memory, hooking it onto the schemas that already exist.

For example: if you have stored and are able to retrieve from your long-term memory that fire is hot and burns, you can hook onto that schema the knowledge that a candle will also be hot and burn. You've extended your existing mental model.

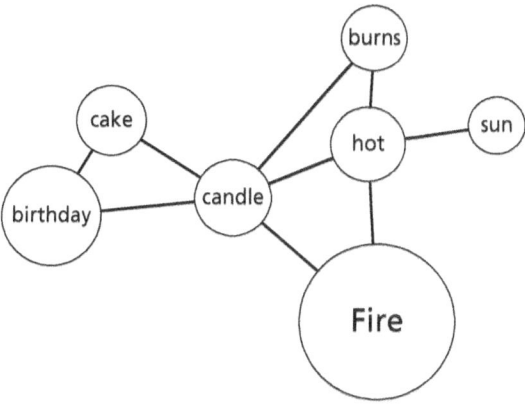

Figure 2 Example of a mental model or schema, located in the long-term memory, based around the concept of fire. You can see how the word "candle" hooks in and extends the pre-existing model.

Figure 2 explains what happens when knowledge is transferred from the limited working memory to the long-term memory. What teachers and other educational professionals need to keep in mind is the limited capacity of working memory. If it is overloaded, pupils will struggle to retain the knowledge required to learn effectively

Teachers must value the complexity of the material, how information is presented and the mental effort required to understand and apply learning.

Put simply: lessons need to be sequenced and tasks broken into smaller steps. Clear worked examples should be provided, extraneous distractions removed and relevant scaffolding, practice and retrieval activities offered. In short, allow pupils to focus on the learning and build up their long-term memory.

## The Oracy Skills Framework

It's also worth mentioning the 2014 work of School 21, the University of Cambridge, and later the national oracy charity Voice 21 and Oracy Cambridge, who partnered to research and develop the *Oracy Skills Framework*. This project was initially funded by the Education Endowment Foundation.

The creators define the framework as follow.

*"The Oracy Skills Framework (OSF) specifies the various skills young people need to develop to deal with a range of different talk situations. The framework has been developed by drawing on available existing resources and research, and in consultation with a range of experts. The OSF is designed to help school leaders, teachers and pupils understand the physical, linguistic, cognitive and social/emotional skills that enable successful discussion, inspiring speech and effective communication."*

**Social and emotional**

Working with others
- Guiding or managing interactions
- Turn-taking

Listening and responding
- Listening and responding appropriately

Confidence in speaking
- Self-assurance
- Liveliness and flair

Audience awareness
- Taking account of level of understanding of the audience

**Cognitive**

Content
- Choice of content to convey meaning and intention
- Building on the views of others

Structure
- Structure and organisation of talk

Clarifying and summarising
- Seeking information and clarification through questioning
- Summarising

Self-regulation
- Maintaining focus on task
- Time management

Reasoning
- Giving reasons to support views
- Critically examining ideas and views expressed

**Linguistic**

Vocabulary
- Appropriate vocabulary choice

Language
- Register
- Grammar

Rhetorical techniques
- Rhetorical techniques such as metaphor, humour, irony and mimicry

**Physical**

Voice
- Pace of speech
- Tonal variation
- Clarity of pronunciation
- Voice projection

Body language
- Gesture and posture
- Facial expression and eye contact

Figure 3 Voice 21 Oracy framework

I frequently refer back to the four strands and the language used within this framework. If you are new to oracy you may want to mark this page for reference!

# Vital threads

Throughout the book I'll return to what I think of as vital threads for achieving effective oracy practice. As the book progresses through different strategies, I'll highlight these threads so you begin to see how they weave through and why they matter.

I have a very varied role – I teach for half the week and I am lucky enough during the other half of the week to visit and support other schools. When I see oracy practice in classrooms or the wider school environment, the following threads are generally what I bear in mind. When I discuss improving oracy practice or provision with schools, it is usually because one of these threads has been forgotten or not prioritised as it should. If there's one takeaway from this book, it's to always keep the following elements in mind.

### Expectations

What are your expectations of the overall outcome? Are they high yet realistic? Does the task genuinely lend itself to oracy? Will the time spent on "teaching to talk" detract from learning, or enrich it? Have you considered the cognitive load of pupils?

### Scaffolds

Consider the scaffolds you currently use in other curriculum areas. What do you provide pupils with to successfully access the learning? What can you consistently provide to encourage participation and clarity of understanding? Teaching dialogically is no different to any of these subject areas.

Always remember that the learning intention is where cognitive load should be focused. If you give pupils seven new sentence stems, they'll spend their energy choosing one, rather than engaging with the intended learning (unless, of course, the lesson is about sentence stems). Cognitive overload often leads to lost focus and low-level disruption.

Scaffolds should be a step towards the learning, not learning in themselves. Ask yourself:

- What do pupils need to access the task?

- What can I put in place to help them reach the expected outcome?

- Can this be part of a generic toolkit, display or resource bank, rather than something I remake every time?

- When can the scaffold be removed?

### Cognitive load

Pupils' cognitive load should be focused on the subject matter. That's why scaffolds exist – to ease the strain on working memory. The same goes for adults: build your oracy strategy bank slowly. You already juggle lessons, behaviour, rewards, medical and safeguarding information, deployment of support staff, and assessment for learning. Don't overload yourself with too many oracy strategies at once. Choose one, practise it until it becomes natural then build from there.

### Modelling

This is key to successful oracy practice and often the most overlooked thread. As an oracy lead, you must model effectively to your staff. I always run staff meetings or CPD sessions in an immersive manner, treating staff as if they are pupils. Immersion is, in my view, the most purposeful form of CPD.

There are several ways teachers can model oracy, each useful in different contexts.

- Immersion in the task with the CPD lead modelling the role of the teacher.

- Teacher to teacher (videoed or live).

- Teacher to teaching assistant.

- Teacher to child.

- Child to child.

- Child to teacher.

### Implementation across the ages

There's a saying: "If you hear a word X times in X different situations, it becomes part of your long-term vocabulary." I see integrating oracy strategies in much the same way. Trial a strategy in one lesson, reflect, refine and try it again – maybe in a new subject or with a different class. Don't give up. I've yet to find an oracy strategy that can't be adapted for any age, subject or ability.

As one secondary English lead put it: "If it's secondary, start with a class you know you can trust. It's scary to let go, and you should only ever do it with a class you feel confident in before trying it elsewhere."

Oracy is for all ages. Yet when research or examples are shared, the younger years are often forgotten. It's easy to imagine a Year 10 discussion, and to adapt it for Year 7 or 6 – but what about Year 1? What does that look like? And what could a Year 9 teacher learn from a Year 1 teacher's strategies?

Every strategy in this book is adaptable and suitable for all ages.

### Manageability

Another misconception is that talk-rich teaching is resource-heavy. While some strategies do require preparation, there are always quick wins that make them manageable.

### Prior learning required

There is a progression of skills that pupils need to take part in oracy-rich learning. Implementation is a slow process – don't run before you can walk. Each strategy in this book highlights the skills pupils need to participate. Pay attention to these basics. Respectful oracy skills matter throughout school and beyond.

### Strategies to embed these skills

Every teacher faces barriers, often daily. This book anticipates some of them and offers suggestions I've found helpful in my own practice.

### Impact

We all enjoy teaching the "nice" lessons, but realistically we need to teach for impact. Often, this impact needs to be measurable. I've tried to highlight the likely impact of each strategy so you know why it's purposeful and how it can elevate learning for *all* pupils.

## A personal turning point

The beauty of oracy, for me, is that there's no single "right way." It isn't a scheme demanding fidelity, it's a set of strategies that become part of your pedagogy and personal style, interwoven into your day as you see their effect on learning.

After being on my own oracy journey for a few years, I remember "teaching" an RE lesson from a plan I hadn't written myself. I'd only skimmed it at lunchtime, and it looked simple. But as I delivered the PowerPoint to Year 1, I noticed passivity. They weren't engaged at all. I may as well have been speaking another language (in fact, that might have been more interesting to them!).

At that moment, my practice shifted. I'd seen the impact of oracy strategies in lessons I'd planned, and I made a conscious choice to adapt all my lessons. I resolved to always ensure pupils understood key vocabulary and had time for purposeful, scaffolded talk. These strategies became second nature, and I began trusting myself to know when and where to use them.

I put "teaching" above in quotes because, to me, this wasn't teaching – it was performing a lesson plan to a passive audience. When a pianist practises, they don't just read the music aloud – they demonstrate understanding through application. A tennis player doesn't improve by only watching Wimbledon. They hit the balls themselves.

Teaching is no different. It is a skill – and one many find terrifying. A teacher should draw on the most effective strategies in their toolkit, not just parrot knowledge.

## Final thoughts

I really hope that when you read this book – whatever age you teach, wherever your school is located and whatever your student body looks like – you approach it with an open mind. Every strategy here can be made relevant from EYFS to key stage 4. You just need to consider the adaptations.

What I'm saying is: if a chapter gives an example from EYFS or key stage 1, please don't just skip ahead. Each chapter ends with tips on applying the strategy to different age groups.

But you know your curriculum, and you know your pupils. Be creative!

# Chapter 1:

## Oracy and me

I turned up at school one morning to be told that I'd been booked onto CPD for the day and needed to quickly make my way there. That session – and the decision to put my name down for it – completely changed the direction of my career (though I had no idea at the time!).

I had been placed in a working party for our local authority, tasked with developing pupils' speaking and listening skills in response to the 2014 National Curriculum's measly nod to their importance. The group's purpose was to create a primary assessment framework designed to highlight gaps in pupils' oracy abilities and understanding of respectful communication, and to provide suggested activities to target these gaps.

I remember sitting in that room – only a few years qualified – surrounded by teachers and leaders who seemed to know exactly what they were talking about. They were discussing research, the curriculum, their opinions…and I felt completely overwhelmed and out of place. Over time, though, that large group of loud, opinionated voices dwindled, leaving behind a wonderful team of passionate teachers who genuinely wanted to understand speaking and listening and give their students the best life chances in a society that didn't always support this.

Looking back, I feel proud to have been part of that forward-thinking group: a diverse collection of enthusiastic teachers with varied expertise, working together to unpick what good speaking and listening really looked like. We researched, identified barriers faced by disadvantaged children and co-created a bank of activities to support teachers in assessing pupils' abilities and planning their development. This gave our pupils a more inclusive way to access their education – something not widely understood or valued at the time.

Those first years of my oracy journey gave me the freedom to explore what speaking and listening meant across different phases. I had space to engage with research and trial ideas in my own classroom. I built a secure foundation for when Voice 21 later entered my life, offering three years of CPD to local Leicester oracy leads.

Engaging with the Voice 21 project was enlightening. It reassured me that the challenges my group and I had been wrestling with for years were being shared and tackled by others. As a teacher, I had never had a 'specialist area' then I discovered the theory and practices of oracy. This really resonated with me and was something I believed in and felt passionate about. It wasn't another scheme or initiative – it just made sense. My whole practice and outlook shifted, and so did the education of the pupils in my class. I began to understand the science of learning more deeply. I recognised pupils' abilities and misconceptions more clearly. Behaviour improved, and my relationships with students flourished.

As my journey continued, I realised that sometimes I saw oracy differently to others. My ideas for implementation weren't always the same, and my natural stubbornness meant I refused to write off a particular strategy just because I taught Year 1. I would always find a way – a scaffold, an adaptation – to make it work and to enhance learning for my pupils.

I believe this is why my passion has continued and why I've been invited to work in different capacities to support with oracy. It's also how the idea for this book came about. I love sharing ideas with colleagues, often apologising when I go off on a roll and throw ten suggestions at colleagues in response to a single question! This book has given me the space to share those ideas without cognitively overloading anyone.

Throughout my career, I've always chosen to work in inner-city schools, often with higher-than-average numbers of pupil premium students. I enjoy rising to the varied challenges these contexts bring and seeing the difference you can make. In these schools, oracy is often a vital priority – and I think that's why I feel most confident embedding it in these settings.

Over time, though, I've realised the challenge of embedding oracy is real in every context. I used to think that schools in more affluent areas, with "well-spoken" children, didn't need to embrace the oracy shift. But working alongside colleagues in those schools opened my eyes. Even in very different contexts and demographics, there are barriers to becoming oracy-rich. All schools need to get on board – and the truth is, they have so much to learn from each other.

# **Chapter 2:**
## Prerequisite skills

## Strategy description

As I began planning each chapter of this book, I noticed certain elements kept repeating. Many strategies relied on the same underlying skills, and common "oracy-related threads" started to appear. One of these was in the pre-skills sections. Quite obviously, many strategies depend on children having a solid grasp of what I'm calling **basic, respectful** oracy skills.

## Context

For any child to engage meaningfully in the social context of oracy, they first need to understand how to be communicative. A common misconception is that this skill develops naturally as children grow, as if it's simply part of their developmental milestones. In reality, children only become successful communicators when these skills are consistently modelled for them and they are immersed in opportunities to practise.

No child wakes up one morning and is suddenly able to count to twenty without prior exposure to numbers. No child learns to swim having never set foot in water, or masters riding a bike after only ever sitting on a swing. Children need exposure, guidance, practice and feedback to understand the mechanics. Speaking, listening, vocabulary and the social-emotional aspects of oracy are no different.

## Implementation

To help children develop a secure understanding of basic, respectful oracy, we must first unpick what this actually means.

Look at Figure 1.1, which shows a blank child drawing. Imagine this child as a canvas.

Figure 1.1 Blank child image

Ask yourself: What do they need, both physically and cognitively, in order to achieve basic, respectful oracy?

Hopefully, you would end up creating an image that specifies the various physical and emotional features a child needs in order to become a respectful communicator.

This image should look something like Figure 1.2.

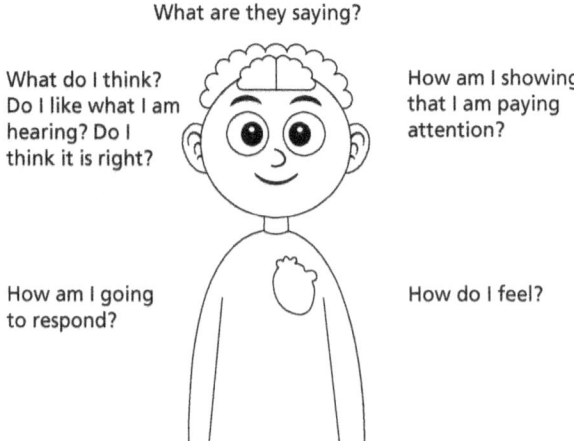

Figure 1.2 Completed child image

By annotating the image, you make visible all the small skills that add up to what I'm calling basic, respectful oracy. (As you can see Figure 1.2 depicts a child who is able to both see and hear. In the chapter on SEND I further discuss adaptations and approaches for pupils who are vision and/or hearing impaired.)

If a child has a basic conversational understanding, this gives them a solid basis for building strong oracy skills. We can begin by teaching that we do not move away when we are communicating with others. We show that we are paying attention, whether by sitting still, looking at the speaker or responding to them. As role models, we must also demonstrate the correct vocal volume. It helps to explain what we are doing as we do it, so pupils can explicitly see and understand.

By this point, children should begin to understand that communication requires eyes and ears. They learn to stay where communication is happening, and they begin to grasp that we use our voices at different levels in different situations. These skills provide a strong foundation for becoming respectful communicators.

There are two further pre-requisite skills I'd add to this list.

1. Turn-taking – making it a non-negotiable in your classroom or school that we do not interrupt or speak over each other.
2. Kindness – ensuring that even when we disagree, we respond with respect.

## Useful scaffolds

These skills need to be modelled for children in all environments, so that they are immersed in respectful communication at all times – not just in the classroom. Think about the wider school context: the office, corridors, playground, dining room and anywhere else where communication happens.

This means all staff need to understand what oracy is and why it matters. It is also crucial that children are praised specifically so they know exactly what they have done well. Phrases like "great listening" or "good oracy" are vague and waste a valuable learning opportunity. Instead, rephrase and add comments, such as:

• "Thank you for looking at me while I was talking – that made me feel listened to."

- "Well done for using the sentence stem in your response – it made your idea clearer."

Specific scaffolds are not as valuable here, because these skills should be the base on which other strategies are built. One simple way to develop these skills without adding to cognitive load is to weave them into your oracy rules (see the example rules at the end of this chapter).

## My own experience

I once had a child in my class who would only ever shout. His natural register was SO LOUD. The poor boy was constantly being told off or reminded to lower his voice.

As a therapeutic practitioner, you learn to step back and consider external factors – something not all teachers do, but which is vital. An obvious starting point would have been to check for a hearing impairment. But when I met his family on the playground, it became clear: there was only ever one volume setting at home, and that was loud. To be heard in that environment, you had to boom your voice – or not bother.

So why would this child automatically change his natural volume without explicit teaching to explain that different settings require different volume levels?

This reinforced my earlier point: children need exposure, guidance, practice and feedback to understand the mechanics of respectful communication.

## Strategies to embed these skills

- Think–Pair–Share
- Ground rules for effective talk
- Effective modelling

## Potential barriers

At the start of the school year, priorities pile up: classroom management, routines, rules, behaviour expectations. Adding oracy to that list can feel like an unnecessary extra. But if you flip your viewpoint to see the potential impact, the benefits quickly outweigh the perceived cost.

Think about it: would you ever skip explicitly teaching your behaviour rules in September just to save time for a different school focus? Of course not. And yet how often do we say, "they just don't/can't listen"? How many times in your career have you actually taught pupils explicitly what listening is and how to achieve it? (For more on this, see chapter 3 Listening.)

## Implementation across the age phases

Every communication opportunity is a chance to practise and consolidate these skills. The difference lies in how we approach them, depending on age and developmental stage. Don't assume older pupils have already mastered them.

In fact, think about some adults you communicate with. Would you honestly say they always tick all of these boxes? If not, we certainly can't assume our pupils will do so automatically!

## Impact

When pupils have a sound understanding of basic, respectful oracy skills, all school talk becomes more positive, thought-provoking and – where appropriate – respectfully challenging. Pupils who develop these foundations will be better equipped to enter the world as empathetic, respectful, well-rounded citizens.

### Basic respectful oracy skills

- Pay attention to the person speaking.
- Show respect and be kind.
- Hear what is being said.
- Have an opinion.
- Use appropriate voice levels.
- Take turns when speaking.

# Chapter 3:
## Listening

According to one estimate, humans typically "spend 70 to 80 percent of our waking hours in some form of communication. Of that time, we spend about 9 percent writing, 16 percent reading, 30 percent speaking, and 45 percent listening." (Lee and Hatesohl, 1983)

## Strategy description

Listening is a severely undervalued skill, often incorrectly assumed to be a natural developmental milestone. It's important to remember that hearing and listening are not the same thing. A child may hear sound, but that does not mean they know how to listen.

Listening is a skill like speaking, reading, writing or number sense: it requires explicit modelling, teaching and guidance. There is no other skill we expect pupils to master without teaching – even play and personal development are taught.

In this chapter, we'll unpick the skills required for listening and consider how these can be explicitly taught in the classroom.

## Context

As the years go by, certain truths become clearer in teaching. For me, the one that resonates most is: you cannot assume prior knowledge or understanding of anything. If we expect pupils to do something – and to do it well – then we must teach it.

My favourite way of explaining why we need to teach listening is to compare it with long division. You are not born knowing how to approach long division, nor do you acquire it through osmosis. It requires explicit teaching and modelling. You would never turn around to a colleague and say, "these pupils just cannot do long division" having never taught them long division – that would be ludicrous!

We are happy to say this about our pupils and listening though!

If pupils do not develop appropriate listening skills, they will struggle to learn and, in turn, they will be less effective at discussing their learning, applying knowledge or connecting it to existing schemas.

## Prior learning required

Success in embedding listening skills depends on pupils having already mastered the basic respectful oracy skills. These ensure pupils know what has been said to them and give them the opportunity to form their own opinions.

## Implementation

Teaching listening is a slow process that must be revisited regularly. Each required skill should be made explicit and discussed in and out of context.

A useful starting point is the Listening Ladder.

In his *Facilitator's and Trainer's Toolkit* (2014), Artie Mahal introduced the concept of "The Listening Ladder". It describes what engaged and effective listening requires.

| | |
|---|---|
| Look at the person speaking to you. | Make eye contact to express that you are interested in what the other person has to say. |
| Ask questions. | Ask follow-up open ended questions to comprehend the meaning of what is being said. |
| Don't interrupt. | Ensure that the interruption is only for clarification of what has been said. |
| Don't change the subject. | You will get an indication to change the topic when the speaker is finished with one thought. Look for cues to transition to another topic. |
| Emotions in control. | Demonstrate this by a gesture such as "nodding your head" so that the speaker gets the message that you are interested in what is being said. |
| Responsive listening. | Through body language such as nodding your head, eyebrow movements, acknowledge that you are just as engaged in the conversation as the speaker is. You can do this without interrupting the speaker by saying "I see…" or "I understand…" |

National oracy charity Voice 21 later developed this model into a framework more suited for schools.

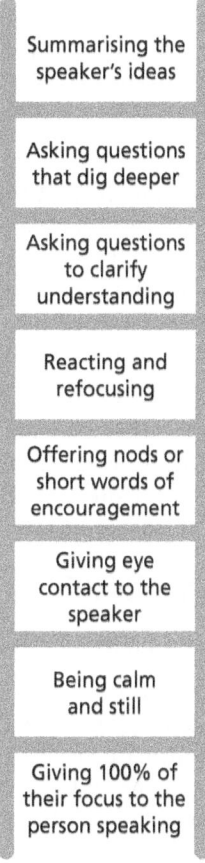

Figure 3.1 Voice 21 Listening ladder

When I work with schools beginning their oracy journey, I always recommend introducing the listening ladder because it's simple, not time-consuming, and effective. The key is to introduce it slowly, one rung at a time, ideally across the whole school. This ensures shared language, feedback and expectations. I often suggest starting with an assembly to provide consistent teaching and introduction.

# Useful scaffolds

Approaches to scaffolding depend on the age of the pupils and your school's context. In my view, the scaffolding comes mainly through teaching, revisiting and building upon the listening ladder in class. For younger pupils, simplify the language and use visuals to support understanding.

# My own experience

Since beginning my oracy journey in 2013 I have always been a champion of listening skills. Personally, I was lucky enough to grow up in a home that deeply valued and respected all voices. My brother and I were always listened to and had great role models, in my parents and their friends, who modelled positive listening behaviours. I have always been surrounded by strong female characters with no-nonsense attitudes so I have never had any reason to doubt the value in my own voice.

I am aware of how lucky I am in this respect, I understand this is not your stereotypical environment to be raised in and that sadly our pupils are often raised in the complete opposite way. How many of your pupils are greeted by a parent looking at their phone?

# Strategies to embed these skills

There are several barriers to embedding listening skills.

- **SEND needs (autism example)**
  I once worked with a teacher who displayed the listening ladder, but her pupils with autism couldn't progress past the "eye contact" step, as they found it uncomfortable. My advice: remove it. The ladder is not a rigid scheme – adapt it to suit your pupils.

- **Hearing or speech impairments**
  Sometimes barriers are beyond our control. What you can control is accessibility: use visual prompts, sentence stems or other supports to ease communication.

- **Cognitive load (pupil context)**
  If a child arrives at school worrying about food at home, they won't focus on listening. Be aware of pupils' personal circumstances and see what you can do to ease their load.

- **Disruptive behaviour**
  Low- or high-level disruption adds extraneous load and breaks listening focus. Rules, routines, respect and consistency are key.

- **Teacher talk**
  Often, the main barrier is **us**. I sympathise with our pupils, I personally have the attention span of a squirrel! When I have to listen for sustained periods I struggle. When working with pupils I follow the "age + 1" rule for minutes of teacher talk. For example, with 7-year-olds, I aim for no more than eight minutes before pupils are actively participating. Break learning into small, focused chunks, punctuated with purposeful talk time.

## Implementation across the age phases

The most common question I get is whether the ladder needs adapting for different ages. My answer has shifted over time. At first, I said no. But as research has evolved, I now see the need to adapt expectations. For example, most 5-year-olds would struggle to summarise conversations – but they can still engage in simpler listening behaviours.

| Artie Mahal | Voice 21 | Ideas for younger pupils |
|---|---|---|
| Look at the person speaking to you. | Give 100% of your attention. | Look at the person who is speaking. |
| Ask questions. | Be calm and still. | Do not interrupt the person speaking. |
| Don't interrupt. | Give eye contact to the speaker. | Show or say how you feel.<br>• "I like that…"<br>• "I agree with…"<br>• "I have been to…" |
| Don't change the subject. | Offer nods or short words of encouragement. | Say what you know or what you thought about when they were speaking.<br>• "I have a…too"<br>• "I have been to…too"<br>• "I remember…" |
| Emotions in control. | React and refocus. | Your body shows the speaker that you are interested: smile, laugh, frown, "Yes!", "Me too!", "Oh no!" |
| Responsive listening. | Ask questions to clarify understanding. | Ask "Why?" or "How?" questions to find out more or to understand. |
| | Ask questions to dig deeper. | |
| | Summarise the speaker's ideas. | |

Below are some ways I have seen the listening ladder presented in different schools. You can see in each image the school has printed the rules out separately. This is because they have introduced them one at a time over a period of time to ensure understanding and meaning. If you just have a small A4 copy of the listening ladder stuck somewhere it is merely collecting dust. If you are displaying listening rules, celebrate them!

Figure 3.2 Listening ladders displayed prominently

## Impact

Quite simply: without awareness of listening, you will not achieve meaningful oracy outcomes. Respectful, effective oracy depends on strong listening foundations.

If you are ready to begin your oracy journey, don't skip listening. Its impact is felt not only in oracy sessions but across every aspect of school life and beyond.

# Chapter 4:
## Sentence stems

## Strategy description

Imagine a flower: without the initial stem, there's nothing for the petals and leaves to bloom from. This strategy works in the same way – you provide students with the "stem" and they grow the rest of the sentence – the "leaves and flower".

Sentence stems (or sentence openers) are a precursor to other oracy strategies. If embedded well, they raise the standard of talk in the classroom and encourage higher-order thinking.

The idea is simple: pupils are shown a few sentence stems and choose the most appropriate one to complete with their own ideas, opinions or answers. These can be displayed in multiple ways – on classroom walls, cards on tables, interactive whiteboards or worksheets.

From a cognitive load theory perspective, stems give pupils a structured way to start their response. This frees up their working memory to focus on the content of the sentence, rather than panicking about how to begin.

Figure 4.1 Example of a Year 2 classroom display of sentence stems

## Context

Sentence stems are versatile. They can be used in any lesson, any subject and any wider school context. Wherever talk happens – which, after reading this book, should be everywhere – sentence stems add value.

## Implementation

The most effective implementation happens when sentence stems are used in two ways, simultaneously.

- **General bank of stems**
  A progressive set of stems displayed in classrooms and shared across the school. This builds a common oracy language and supports language development year on year.

- **Subject-specific stems**
  Tailored to the lesson. For example:

  - General: "I agree…"

  - Art: "I can see the artist has…"

  - History: "The Industrial Revolution changed lives because…"

Subject-specific stems keep pupils on-topic, reassure less confident pupils and reduce off-topic wandering.

Over time, stems can also be introduced in wider school contexts.

| | |
|---|---|
| On display boards around the school (best to keep the tone positive!) | • "These children have been learning…"<br>• "This display reminds me of…"<br>• "The most interesting part of this display is…"<br>Ideas for EYFS, early reading pupils, EAL or SEND:<br>• "I can see…"<br>• "I like…"<br>• "There are…" |
| In the main school hall | I would suggest using the progressive sentence stems displayed on classroom walls. Revisiting this language with pupils when they are within the assembly/PE environment further consolidates the school's shared oracy language. This hopefully begins to demonstrate to pupils that wherever we are, we have opinions, and therefore will need to remember that we agree and disagree respectfully (not a bad reminder to have within PE lessons!). |
| Near communication points with office staff, premises officers, hygiene assistants or other colleagues with whom pupils may not speak to regularly | • "Excuse me…"<br>• "Please could I…"<br>• "Would you…"<br>• "Thank you for…"<br>(It does not harm anyone to encourage manners and respect.) |
| Entrance and exit points of rooms or buildings | • "Good…" (encourage use of names)<br>• "Thank you…"<br>• "I hope you have / had…" |

This reinforces the message that talk is everywhere and that pupils should communicate respectfully in all contexts.

## Prior learning required

The only prerequisite is the understanding that full sentences have more impact than one-word utterances. Sentence stems are part of the oracy "building blocks", and even non-readers can access them with visual prompts.

## Useful scaffolds

- For less confident pupils: laminated "safe" stems ("I can see…", "I like…", "I notice…") which they keep to hand.

- For more confident pupils: challenge stems ("Let me give you three reasons…", "On one hand…but on the other hand…").

- Visual prompts: help both non-readers and pupils with high cognitive load.

## My own experience

Sentence stems were one of my personal oracy lightbulb moments. They showed me that talk could be purposeful when structured.

Early in my career, I often used "turn and talk" as a filler when I needed a quick break or had a technical issue. But then I discovered that if I put up a concept cartoon alongside simple stems like "I agree…" or "I disagree…", pupils were suddenly reasoning and arguing their points – on task, on topic and engaged.

Another breakthrough came with visual representation. Showing an image from a previous lesson and pairing it with stems like "I remember…" or "This makes me think…" created a simple but powerful Assessment for Learning (AfL) tool.

Knowledge Representation + Sentence Stems = Lightbulb Moment!

## Strategies to embed these skills

- Reading ability: stems may be inaccessible without visuals.

- Limited vocabulary: pupils may struggle to finish stems; you can support this with word banks or providing prompts from previous learning.

- Cognitive overload: too many stems (e.g. huge laminated cards) distract from curriculum content. Oracy should elevate learning, not detract from it.

# Implementation across the age phases

| EYFS | Stems can be pictorial or symbol-based, (you may wish to use Widgit or similar tools). |
|------|----------------------------------------------------------------------------------------|
| KS1 | Sentence stems must be appropriate for pupils' ability, both in reading and cognitively. Ensure the language you use is not pitched at a level that is too high. Sentence stems must not be an additional barrier to pupils achieving success. |
| KS2 | I have been into classrooms where pupils are sat with double-sided A4 laminated cards providing all the sentence stems you need for life! As you can imagine there was so much consideration going into which one to select that the curriculum content was pushed aside and the learning objective was far from being met. Oracy must be a tool to elevate learning, not detract from it. |
| KS3 | Sentence stems need to be used to encourage higher order thinking. Provide opportunities to engage with new and interesting vocabulary and moments to elicit in-depth dialogue, and broach contentious points while maintaining a respectful, open and safe environment. |
| SEND | I have worked alongside a colleague who runs a specialist provision for pupils with autism and during all CPD I lead we end up discussing how we can adapt the subject matter in her context. This particular leader has enthusiastically embraced sentence stems in her area. Her most successful sentence stem? "It is…". This is predominantly used in her morning routine of naming the day and identifying the current weather. This may sound simple but this has encouraged phrases and simple sentences with her pupils rather than single word answers. |

| EAL | Sentence stems for our EAL pupils may also need setting up a pictorial vocabulary bank. This allows the opening to be provided and the pupil to select the ending but without the additional cognitive load required when translating, retrieving unfamiliar nouns and verbs, constructing the sentence and then verbalising this in English.<br>For example: "A good friend…"<br><br>Adding an incorrect visual image as a decoy provides you with an additional AfL opportunity. |

## Impact

Over time, pupils repeatedly exposed to stems may internalise them into their inner dialogue. This means they will begin to write with the same structured reasoning – reducing workload for exam and coursework prep. Sentence stems become embedded in their mental models, ready to draw on across all subjects.

Sentence stem banks

## SEND provision

- It is...
- It has...
- I have...
- I am...

## Nursery / Foundation Stage 1

- It is...
- It has...
- I have...
- I am...
- I like...
- I can...

## Reception / Foundation Stage 2

- I think...
- I know...
- I notice...
- I agree...
- I disagree...
- It is...
- It is not...
- They are...
- They are the same because...
- They are not the same because...
- They are different because...
- I like...
- I don't like...
- It is...
- It has...
- It will...
- I will...

## Key Stage 1

Consider progression from beginning of Year 1 to summer of Year 2.

- I think that...because...
- I know...because...
- I agree because...
- I disagree because...
- I like...because...
- I don't like...because...
- I noticed...
- It makes me think...
- X's idea made me think...
- In my opinion...
- They are the same because...
- They are different because...
- They are similar because...
- They are alike because...

## Key Stage 2

Consider this progression to build slowly from the beginning of Year 3 to the summer of Year 6. These sentence stems aim to build pupil's confidence and extend their reasoning, prediction and comparison skills. Pupils are encouraged to practise adding "because" and to link ideas and knowledge.

- I think that…because… and also…
- I know this is true because…
- I noticed that…which shows…
- This is similar to…because…
- This is different from… because…
- I agree with X because…
- I disagree with X because…

- Another idea could be…
- This reminds me of…
- I predict that…because…
- I would explain this as…
- This is important because…
- I can compare this to…
- I wonder if…
- I might change my mind if…

## Key Stage 3 +

This progression is aimed to build slowly from the beginning of Year 7 and continue building. These sentence stems aim to introduce *evaluative* language into the pupils' discussion, encourage alternative viewpoints, allow more abstract connections and weigh up significance or relevance.

- In my opinion, the most important point is…because…
- On the other hand…
- A possible explanation could be…
- This suggests that…
- This could be interpreted as…
- I can support this idea with evidence from…
- I might challenge this idea because…

- Another perspective to consider is…
- This connects to…because…
- I could argue that…although…
- The consequence of this is…
- This highlights…
- It is significant that…
- I would summarise this as…
- Ultimately, I think…because…

# **Chapter 5:**
## Vocabulary focus

*"While key vocabulary is identified and taught, this is not necessarily embedded through repeated practice in different contexts. Often, pupils do not remember to use the vocabulary in their written and spoken language."*
*Telling the Story: The English Education Subject Report (Ofsted, 2024)*

## Strategy description

A vocabulary focus is about deconstructing learning to the bare bones and asking: which words are absolutely vital for pupils to succeed? These words are the key to unlocking both understanding and application.

This isn't a strategy you can just pick up and run with. It's more like a scaffold for other strategies – a foundation that makes them successful. The process works best when broken into small, deliberate steps. Tom Sherrington's WalkThru (2020) on deliberate vocabulary development is a useful reference here and has been a helpful starting point when I've worked with colleagues.

|  | What? | Tip |
|---|---|---|
| Step one | Unpick the vocabulary that is the key to pupils achieving success **and** specify on lesson plans for all teachers to be aware of. | These words should be key to unlocking deep understanding. (Tier 2 words – see below) |
| Step two | Plan for the explicit teaching of these words, There are many activities that you could include or use – see resources bank for ideas and inspiration. | Try not to introduce too many words at once. Drip feed at points that are appropriate. At this point you should also ensure you know the definition you will use. |

|  | What? | Tip |
|---|---|---|
| Step three | Find a visual image to keep alongside the word. | Consider cognitive load when selecting or creating images. They must clearly represent what you are depicting. |
| Step four After explicit teaching | How will this vocabulary be transferred into pupils' long term memories? Plan for retrieval, revisiting and re-learning. | What happens to this word now? |

Tier 2 words are the words that are essential for pupils' success across the curriculum. They can be applied and used in a wide range of subjects and contexts. Examples include words such as "compare", "consequence", "justify" and "significant". These words require deliberate teaching and repeated practice. They need to be revisited often, modelled in talk and used in meaningful contexts.

Tier 2 words don't stick after just one encounter. Children need to hear them, say them, practise them, reuse them and apply them. That's why oracy matters. Vocabulary grows through talk and experience.

Teaching with a deliberate focus on tier 2 vocabulary does not just improve reading or writing skills – it gives pupils the language they need to understand, think, form opinions, make links and learn.

## Context

When we talk about "vocabulary," people often mean very different things. For teachers, though, it's a concern in nearly every classroom. Vocabulary knowledge, understanding and acquisition is quite often the hidden barrier behind misconceptions. It's where carefully planned lessons and assessments can fail.

It's now widely acknowledged that learning sticks when the "new" knowledge hooks onto pupils' existing mental models. Those models hinge, ultimately, on a child's range and depth of vocabulary. When you witness one of those lightbulb moments – when a word finally clicks and unlocks an idea – it suddenly becomes easier to understand what pupils are grappling with and where barriers lie.

## Implementation

This approach isn't quick or easy, but it's absolutely worth it. To do it well, you need to invest time in combing through your curriculum, identifying the tier 2 words children need and planning for them explicitly.

Involve the staff who teach the subject matter – they know what actually gets taught, how pupils respond and where the barriers crop up. Sometimes those barriers come from vocabulary, sometimes from unnecessary subject knowledge, sometimes from the way something has always been explained. Teachers also know which words are already embedded and which never get touched. Their insight stops you adding words for the sake of it.

The conversations you have while doing this are invaluable. Is that word really tier 2, or is it actually tier 3? Is there a more useful alternative? Vocabulary selection is subjective, and having multiple perspectives challenges assumptions and can improve outcomes.

## Prior learning required

When we think about vocabulary, we often jump straight to the new words pupils need. But we can forget that this depends on secure tier 1 vocabulary – and the real-life experiences to back it up.

If children haven't *experienced* plunging into water, how will they grasp the words "splash" or "dive"? If they've never stood on sand, how do they picture "gritty" or "grainy"?

Without lived experiences, pupils have no mental model to attach new words to. Research shows that if there's nothing to "stick to," vocabulary won't stick.

A simple but powerful example: a Year 2 class went on a "litter pick" as part of a science topic on caring for the environment. The teacher handed out black bags and litter pickers, expecting enthusiasm. Instead, most children stared at the ground looking puzzled. One child even tried to prise up the pavement! Why? Because they didn't know the word "litter". They thought they were looking for *glitter*.

Had the teacher stopped to unpick potentially tricky vocabulary beforehand, that barrier would never have derailed the lesson.

## Colleague insight

Paul, the English lead for a multi-academy trust, and a secondary English and oracy specialist, reflected on his own learning:

"I kept encouraging open discussion, but pupils never reached the point I wanted them to. I eventually realised I wasn't *adding* enough scaffolds or parameters. Once I introduced sentence stems, key vocabulary and clearer stimuli, the talk suddenly had direction. Without those supports, pupils went on tangents. With them, they were focused and purposeful."

This is such an important reminder: it isn't just about encouraging talk – it's about shaping it.

## Useful scaffolds

- **Visuals**
  Always provide one, especially when pupils don't already have a mental model. That might be a real object, a photo, clipart or even your own drawing.

- **Crib sheets**
  A simple list of target words with accompanying images gives pupils something to reference during tasks.

- **Planned definitions**
  Have pupil-friendly definitions ready so you aren't caught improvising.

- **Retrieval**
  Vocabulary isn't one-and-done. You need to revisit words in new contexts, across subjects, and over time.

One of my favourite vocabulary retrieval activities came when I was planning a literacy lesson on *Little Red Riding Hood*. The class had already learned words like cottage, fearless, sly, cunning, timid, woodcutter. I put the list into AI and asked it to generate an image using those words. The next day, pupils studied the picture and identified the words they recognised. It was a fantastic AfL moment: some children spotted the words confidently, others revealed gaps.

Later, I planned to adapt this by creating "spot the difference" images or weaving new words into the same picture. It's such a simple way to keep vocabulary alive.

## My own experience

I've seen some unforgettable misconceptions when vocabulary wasn't unpacked properly.

During a shared reading of Roald Dahl's 1978 book *The Enormous Crocodile* I asked pupils to highlight words they didn't know. One child chose "croc". When I asked what he pictured, he admitted he thought it meant a giant Croc° shoe floating down the river – greedy and brave! Without that vocabulary check, he could have spent the whole unit misunderstanding the text, and I might never have realised.

More recently, I mentored an ECT teaching a computing lesson on digital photography. Pupils were happily suggesting unicorns and rainbows to "improve" their photos – fun, but completely missing the objective. The focus should have been on words like "filters", "focus", "lighting" and "positioning". We reflected afterwards that a simple vocabulary bank on the board would have grounded the talk and made the assessment opportunity crystal clear.

## Strategies to embed these skills

Time is always the barrier. Vocabulary doesn't come with neat data points, so it often gets pushed aside in favour of measurable objectives. But I would argue, based on the crocodile vs. Croc° example, that if pupils don't understand the vocabulary, they won't succeed anyway. The vocabulary *is* the learning.

The time investment doesn't have to be huge. I build it into planning: every foundation subject starts with a quick vocabulary slide to revisit old words and introduce new ones. In literacy, I dedicate a specific lesson in the exploratory stage to vocabulary. That way, it isn't shoehorned in – it has space to breathe.

## Implementation across the age phases

Adaptation across phases is about balance – choosing the right words and the right strategies for your class. And always, *limit the number of new words*. Think about how many **you** could learn and retain at once. Children are no different.

| Strategy | How |
|---|---|
| Draw the word | As simple as it sounds! Get a whiteboard and a pen and show me what is in your head. This is such a valuable AfL strategy. This allows you to see if pupils understand or indeed if they have nothing to share at this point. |
| Spot the word | Share an image or bank of images and see if the pupils can spot the word you are looking at. |
| Matching | Provide target vocabulary and a bank of images for children to match. |
| Placing the word in context | Introduce by sharing a story, poem, song or other way of pupils seeing or experiencing the word in a real or meaningful context or situation. |
| Share the word alongside similar words or similar spellings | Show a group of words that includes your new word, where all of the words in the group have the same meaning. |
| Acting or moving | The best way to illustrate this is teaching "pounce". I had two children act out the cat and mouse. Whenever we then referenced "pounce" in the future the children were able to reference this teaching. |
| Use a book, video, song or experience | In addition to the acting or moving strategy above for the word "pounce", another idea would be to share a video in a real context of a different animal pouncing. This would help to link to real contexts for the pupils. Alternatively you could share a video that depicts a few animals pouncing and see if pupils are able to spot these. |
| Find a personal connection | We had a child turn up on PE day in his comfy tracksuit. Luckily this was also the day that "casual" appeared within phonics. We were able to explain that this child had come to school in his "casual" clothes and used this to add meaning to this word. When we revisited this word later on in the term the pupils remembered it by the personal connection we had made. |

| Strategy | How |
|---|---|
| Vocabulary bullseye | One of my favourite vocabulary strategies.<br><br>land · sea · country · Edinburgh · England · capital city · London · north, south, east, west · Scotland · Cardiff · Belfast · Northern Ireland · Wales<br><br>You can add images to the words to reduce cognitive load for pupils.<br>This can be used in so many different ways to aid both speakers and listeners.<br>As a rehearsal pupils could use it on their own to practise. They could use it with a partner – how many can the partners say as they discuss? How many does their partner say?<br>Pupils could sit in a small group and one member tracks within the discussion how many of the words get used. One of the most effective ways is, while a presenter speaks, the listening pupils track which words have been used. I enjoy using this strategy in this way as it ensures accountability for all, all pupils engaged at all times. |

These activities make vocabulary visible, active and accountable.

## Impact

We may not be able to measure vocabulary growth neatly on a spreadsheet, but its impact is undeniable. A broad vocabulary deepens curriculum understanding, reduces frustration in communication and helps children navigate social interactions with more ease.

It's also vital in our increasingly diverse classrooms. EAL pupils, for instance, often arrive with a strong tier 1 vocabulary in their home language. As their English grows, so will their vocabulary – EAL is not a barrier.

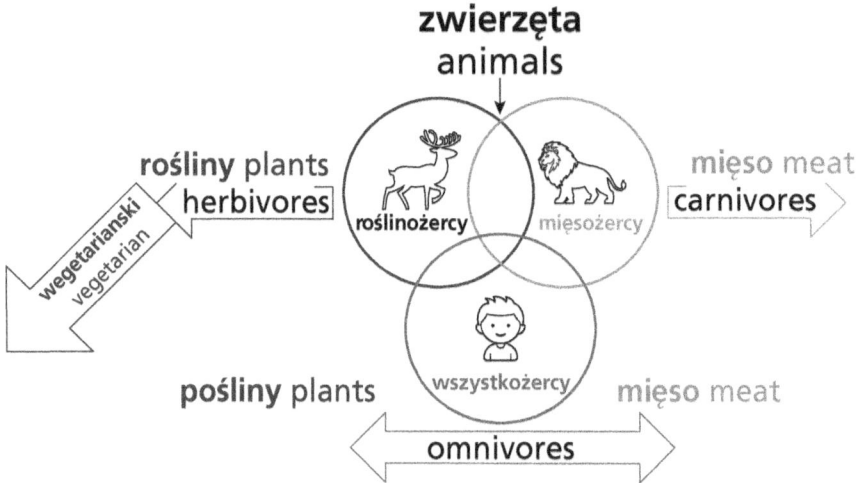

Figure 5.1 Example of a mental model of an EAL pupil – Polish and English

You can see from Figure 5.1 representation that the mental model of an EAL pupil is rich in language. In contrast to this, imagine a model that has no basic language or words – that would be where the barrier occurs!

In contrast with an EAL pupil, children whose first language is English but who have had limited spoken interaction at home often arrive with much weaker schemas. Those pupils need deliberate, explicit vocabulary teaching more than anyone.

And that's why vocabulary focus isn't optional – it's essential.

# Chapter 6:
## Vocabulary jars

## Strategy description

The idea of a vocabulary jar is exactly as simple as it sounds – a jar, sitting proudly in your classroom, collecting the words that really matter for learning. Over the course of the year it fills up with the tier 2 words children have been explicitly taught and actually used. At any point, whenever you've got a minute between transitions, you can dip into it. A child (or you) pulls out a word, and then the fun starts:

- What does it mean?

- Where have you heard it before?

- What does it remind you of?

From there, you can go deeper – synonyms, antonyms, linked subject vocabulary…the possibilities really are endless.

## Context

At the start of my oracy journey, I was part of a brilliant little team – all as enthusiastic as me, and spread across the school phases. That gave us a really clear view of what oracy looked like, from EYFS right through to Year 6. Our corridor conversations, staffroom chats and CPD sessions constantly celebrated the tiny wins and picked apart the barriers. The buzz was real, and it wasn't just us who felt it.

The school I was in at the time had almost two-thirds of pupils eligible for Pupil Premium. Our drive was simple: we wanted every child leaving Year 6 to be at least at the expected level, if not higher. But their starting point was tough. Baseline communication in EYFS was nowhere near where it "should" be.

As staff, we shared a common belief, best stated in Thompson's (2022) book about Ron Berger:

*"It is our fundamental responsibility to give children the chance to be excellent."*

And that meant levelling the playing field.

The second big barrier was one that teachers everywhere will recognise: so many pupils lack the vocabulary and life experiences needed to properly access the curriculum. Ron Berger talks about teachers honing their craft and being determined to find success for their pupils, and as Thompson reminds us: "I could do more to affect change in my students."

It's true. Vocabulary starts at home, and if a child doesn't hear rich, varied language there, they'll inherit those limits. Some families provide that naturally through talk, books and experiences. Others simply can't.

A story that has always stuck with me came from a colleague:

*"I went on a school trip to the farm and one of the parents volunteering hadn't heard of a goat before. They told all the children it was a small horse!"*

That's why we have to take responsibility for making vocabulary explicit in schools.

I've kept lists of surprising words children didn't know across different year groups…things you'd assume would be secure. They weren't.

| Goat (Reception) | Nest (Reception) | Hedge (Year 2) |
| Uniform (Reception) | Ladybird (Year 1) | Journey (Year 2) |
| Caterpillar (Reception) | Litter (Year 1) | Path (Year 2) |
| Squirrel (Reception) | Clown (Year 1) | Paws (Year 5) |

One of the most exciting moments in the early days of my oracy journey was when Nadia, a fantastic EYFS teacher, introduced a "vocabulary jar" to her Reception children. She'd read about it online, gave it a go and saw that it had a huge impact. Honestly, if you only take *one* strategy from this book – make it this one. I promise you'll see a difference.

## Implementation

One school I worked with tackled the problem of assessing foundation subjects by focusing on vocabulary. The thinking was: if children can retain the words, use them in context and connect them to other knowledge, then they've shown secure understanding.

Each subject leader created a vocabulary bank of nine tier 2 words for every unit of study. These were selected carefully, linked directly to curriculum endpoints and national objectives. They were explicitly taught, revisited, displayed – and then, crucially, placed into the vocabulary jar at the end of the unit.

Figure 6.1 Word jar

Here's the beauty of it: when you revisit those words by pulling them from the jar, you're not just checking recall. You're inviting children to say:

- "I remember when we learned this word…"
- "It makes me think of…"
- "We used it in geography when…"

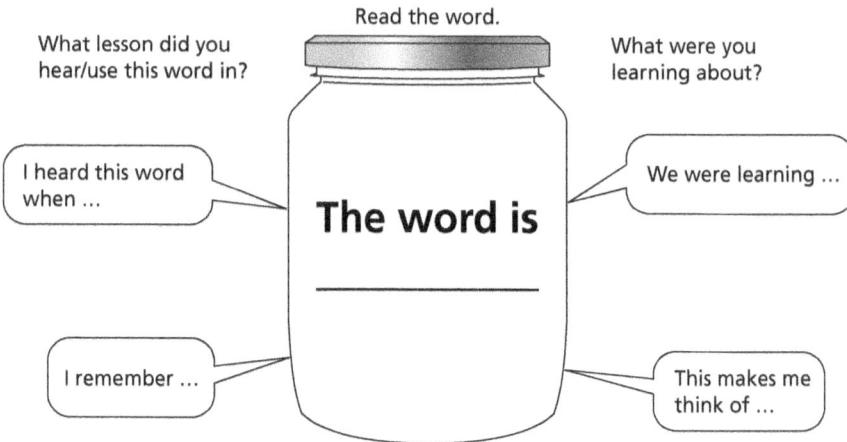

Figure 6.2 Word jar activity

That's retrieval. That's metacognition. And it's fun.

You can keep it visual for younger pupils (swapping "I" for "we" in stems to encourage pair talk), or challenge older ones to make links across subjects.

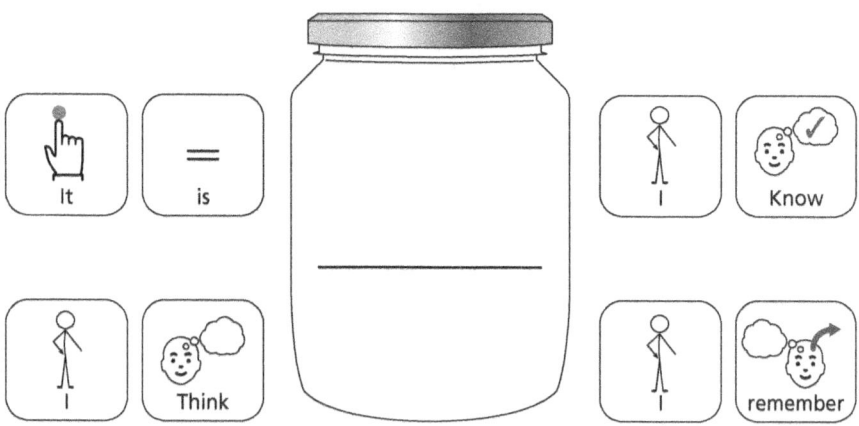

Figure 6.3 Visual word jar activity

Subject leaders can also use the jars during monitoring. If the target vocabulary has genuinely been taught well, pupils should be able to explain it, use it and link it back to their subject knowledge.

## Useful scaffolds

Two essentials for this are:

- An image – to anchor meaning.

- A clear definition, planned in advance so you don't improvise something confusing or Google something embarrassing!

This way, staff across year groups are consistent, and misconceptions are avoided. Personally, I love using drama too – get children to act out words. It sticks.

## My own experience

In my own school, every class has a vocabulary jar. Teachers drop in the targeted tier 2 words at the end of each topic, and over time the jars fill with a rich mix of words from across the curriculum.

### Geography

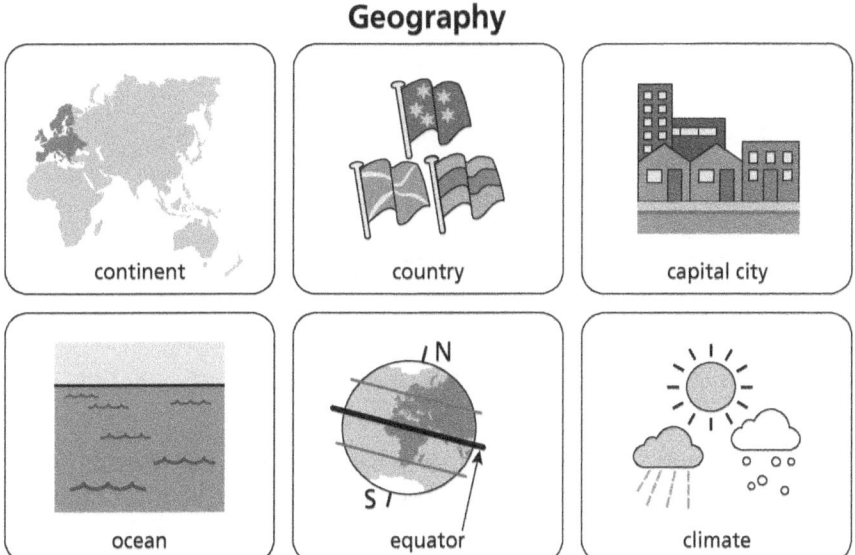

Figure 6.4 Geography words

These words are mixed in with words from other subjects, units or topics from both their current academic year and the preceding years. As the targeted tier 2 words are prescribed from subject leads it does not matter if these pupils are mixed up, as their jar will still have the same content.

# Geography

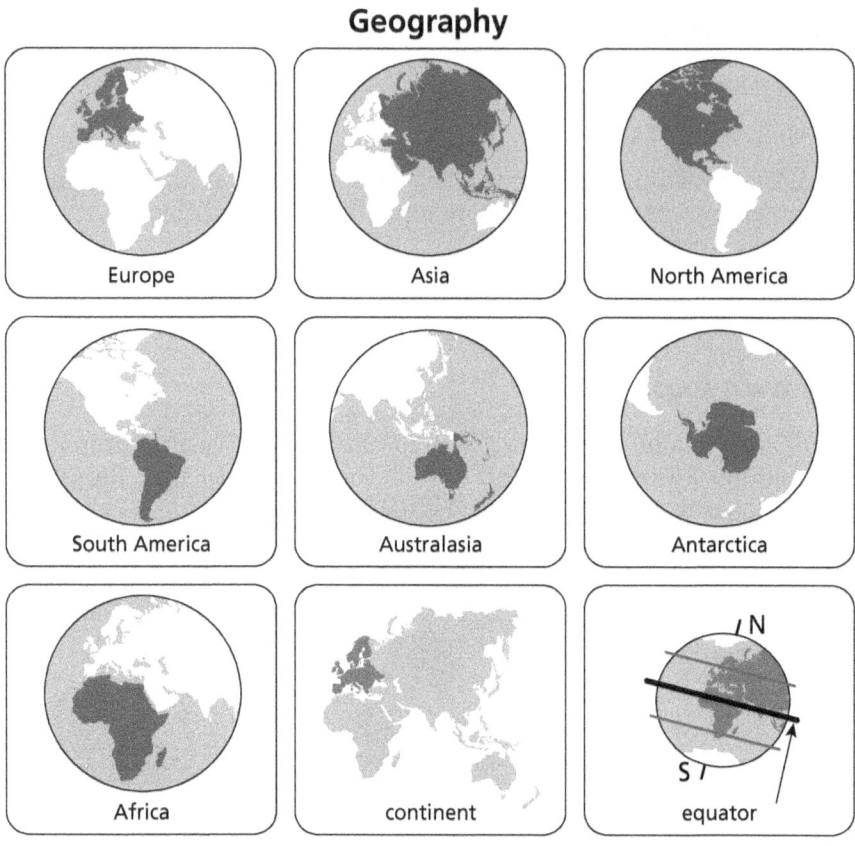

Figure 6.5 Expanded geography words

You can see on this grid that two words have been revisited but the other words add onto prior knowledge that the children have.

When those words are pulled out, sentence stems support discussion and help pupils show what they know. I've heard some brilliant examples in pupil voice sessions:

*"Continent. I remember this from geography. We learned the 7 continents, sang a song and even had the hall turned into a giant world map. Antarctica was blue cones and PE mats because it's icy and cold. That's how I remember it's south of the equator."*

That's the kind of retrieval and contextual understanding we're aiming for.

## Strategies to embed these skills

Of course, there are barriers – and time is the biggest one. Time to choose the words, update the jar and use it in lessons. But here's my honest view: oracy isn't about strict fidelity to a scheme. Every explicit moment you can find for vocabulary is a win. Don't beat yourself up if the jar isn't perfectly updated every week.

## Implementation across the age phases

The key words here are: visuals, quantity, cognitive load and relevance. If these are considered when creating resources or selecting words for jars you will provide pupils with a strong selection of vocabulary.

| Visuals | This seems like the obvious adaptation for younger children but its uses span further than that. All new vocabulary introduced to pupils should be done visually to help them build a richer understanding. The visual helps as a prompt to remember and also as a base for where the word will link into the pupils' mental models. Giving a visual is similar to looking at the root word: what do we know and what can we infer? |
|---|---|
| Quantity | How many new words are you introducing to your vocabulary jar at a time? Are the children able to retain that quantity of knowledge in their working memory? Would it be beneficial to share less words to aim for greater levels of understanding and retention? |
| Cognitive load | What is the current load on pupil's cognition at this point? How much new information have they been expected to learn and understand already and what additional capacity do you feel they have? |
| Relevance | How much of the new vocabulary you are sharing is absolutely needed and relevant for the children to understand the lesson content? Are you adding additional and unnecessary cognitive load? Could you be savvy about which words you select to put into the jar to aid retrieval but free up working memory capacity? |

## Impact

All the research tells us the same thing: vocabulary is one of the strongest predictors of later success. Oracy and vocabulary go hand in hand.

As Voice 21 (2026) puts it:

*"Oracy is the responsibility of every teacher and the entitlement of every child."*

And Neil Mercer (2025) reminds us:

*"You are the only second chance for some children to have a rich language experience. If these children are not getting it at school, they are not getting it."*

Vocabulary jars might look simple, but they are one way we can give children that chance.

# **Chapter 7:**
## Oracy assemblies

## Strategy description

In a school day, where every minute counts and our aim is for pupils to be engaged in learning, is twenty minutes of passive listening really the best use of time? Those minutes can be re-purposed to support curriculum delivery, develop pupils personally and make space for explicit oracy teaching. I'd call that a win–win.

## Context

I'll be honest: like every teacher, I enjoy delivering pupils to assembly and grabbing fifteen minutes to reset and breathe. But if we're serious about giving pupils the best education, we need to ask whether the traditional assembly is fit for purpose in a world where we value cognitive load and working schemas.

Put yourself in a pupil's shoes. You're fully engaged in maths. Then, you're moved to the hall and spoken at for twenty minutes about an unrelated topic, with unfamiliar vocabulary. Likely outcomes?

- You switch off (and behaviour may slip).
- You try to keep up and get frazzled or form misconceptions.

If you reflect honestly on your assembly audience, are your hard-to-reach pupils accessing the content? How many learners leave with the understanding you hoped for? Probably not a majority.

## Prior learning required

The most successful oracy assemblies sit on a foundation of basic, respectful oracy skills (listening, body language, voice levels, turn-taking and kindness). Without these, the hall becomes noisy and chaotic.

Also consider your intent. Wanting a "wow" strategy is different from embedding a culture of talk to improve understanding and outcomes. The latter mindset tends to lead to deeper success.

## Implementation (and my own experience)

To me it is so special and so interesting that the beauty of an oracy assembly is that there is not one "correct" way to do it. The format you choose will depend on:

- School context.
- Behaviour and engagement.
- School improvement priorities.
- Number of available adults.
- Pupils' current oracy abilities.

You could have one teacher in the middle with all the pupils around in a circle and other adults at the side, small groups at tables or on the floor, a circle with children in the middle and all teachers outside...any variation is possible.

The commonalities between these setups is that the children are all able to face both the teacher facilitating and their group easily. Where adults are available they are actively involved in the discussions, not just observing.

### A predictable weekly flow

A consistent structure reduces anxiety and supports success, especially for less-confident pupils.

On entry: display a familiar talking prompt (image, retrieval question). Pupils already have prior knowledge and vocabulary, so they can start talking immediately as they arrive.

Home pre-share (optional but powerful): post the prompt on your parent comms beforehand. Families can discuss it (in home languages if they wish). Pupils then arrive ready to contribute – particularly helpful for quieter children who can begin by sharing a family member's view. This allows the pupil to be less responsible for this opinion and therefore they are not as self aware.

Set the tone: recap your oracy rules and name the target skill(s) for this assembly. Do any explicit oracy teaching needed here.

### Oracy detectives

Select two to four Oracy Detectives. They circulate and look for pupils who are following the target rules (listening, body language, respectful turn-taking, sentence stems, etc.). At the end, each detective names one Oracy Star and explains why, with specific oracy evidence.

Why Oracy Detectives and not Talk Detectives? Because oracy is more than talking: it includes listening, social and physical elements.

### Four-stage oracy assembly

## Stage 1: Spark the talk

Show an image (or very short clip) that provokes curiosity, empathy or gentle controversy. Around it, display target stems and/or vocabulary.

Example stems:

- "I think..."
- "I know..."
- "They are feeling..."
- "If that were me..."

Feedback routine: invite contributions. Contributors stand (if willing) and peers track the speaker (body and eyes). I once feared this was too demanding, but pupils quickly wanted to stand – because the environment was calm, supportive and opinion-friendly. I do allow hands up here to gauge who wants to speak (although I'll still cold-call thoughtfully when appropriate).

> On a personal note, I initially trialled these assemblies with 120 KS1 pupils – solo! It wasn't perfect on week one, but by week six our SIP happened to pop in and what she saw left her impressed. Later, I involved the wider oracy team and this helped to grow the assemblies further.

## Stage 2: Add context

Layer in information to deepen understanding (facts, short reading, concise data, a model answer, a quick clip). Figure 7.1 shows an example.

Figure 7.1 Cyber safety tips

### Stage 3: Apply and connect

Bring it all together. Ask pupils to apply new understanding to a real context (class, school, community, online). Link to school values/British values to add more of a personal meaning.

### Stage 4: Celebrate and close

Oracy Detectives share specific praise. The teacher names what went well and one next-step focus for talk. A calm exit routine (e.g. two deep breaths, quiet "thank-you" to group partners) helps reset.

## Useful scaffolds

No special "assembly-only" scaffold is required here if you're already using:

- Oracy rules (visible and revisited).
- Sentence stems (progressive, age-appropriate).
- Oracy Detectives (with a prompt sheet).
- Vocabulary banks (target words on screen).

These familiar tools and routines make oracy transferable from classroom to hall.

## Strategies to embed these skills

- **Space**
  Halls are busy. Plan flexible layouts that still allow group talk and visibility.

- **Entry/exit routines**
  Teach them explicitly. End with a calming reset so chatter doesn't spill out.

- **Noise**
  Use clear group sizes (2–4), set voice levels, rehearse "talk stop" signal.

- **Adult deployment**
  Brief adults so they are involved and keep groups on task. Occasionally it needs pointing out that the adult is there as a valuable oracy role model.

- **Confidence**
  Begin with low-stakes prompts and lean on pre-shared home discussion.

## Implementation across the age phases

One of the proudest moments of my career was during my time learning about oracy through Voice 21. We were part of a group of enthusiastic teachers from around Leicester who were all passionate and very onboard. This group had a wide range of participants from all age phases and school contexts. Over time we got to know each other and what each of us was trialling back in our own schools, learning from each other – it was a really positive experience. There were a few people really interested in how my assemblies were going and it became a joke as to who else had dared to run one in their school. Paul, the English lead for a multi-academy trust, and a secondary English and oracy specialist, and one of my contributors, was part of this conversation and every time admitted that he had still not dared. I was amazed by this as he worked in a secondary school. I couldn't understand how I had had a go with five-, six- and seven-year-olds but he was scared to try with older pupils!

In the end we decided that he needed to come and observe my KS1 assembly to see what it logistically looked like. I do not see the age barrier when it comes to oracy and the different strategies you can use – hence this book – but it was seen by others as a wild idea that he might gain something from seeing such a different phase.

Paul said:

*"I started with Year 11 because they were my comfort year. Then Year 7... Year 9...Soon staff were asking to be booked in.*

*We co-planned and delivered together. The big 'wow' was seeing 220 Year 11s engaged in structured conversation – proof of what scaffolds and purpose can do.*

*It showed me students want to talk and engage. Give them the opportunity and they rise to it. Oracy isn't an add-on – it improves teaching, learning and school life."*

Sometimes the key to unlocking confidence is simply seeing it done, even in a different phase.

## Impact

Since I started these assemblies in 2019 I have had some epic, stand out, pupil moments. One year I had a child in Year 1 who stood up and reduced staff to tears with his feedback about his future self. He explained that he wanted to work hard at school to achieve a good job, he wanted to get a good job so he could earn lots of money. He then said the reason he wanted lots of money was to give it all to charities which help very sick children. Never, would you have expected this particular child to come out with that response.

Another special moment was having a Year 2 child with sensory sensitivity and elective mutism participate in the assembly. For the majority of the year this pupil sat silently and would not participate. He was not distracting others or misbehaving, he just seemed passive, until one day in the summer term he raised his hand to feedback. This pupil did not stand up to contribute but spoke clearly about their opinion to all the other pupils sitting in the hall. This, to me, was such a proud moment! It had taken him nearly a year to build up the confidence in himself to believe in his own voice!

One final proud moment I have to share was seeing one of our pupils who came from our DSP (Designated Specialist Provision) who was very anxious and very quiet, raise her hand and stand to contribute so clearly that all her peers could hear her – she had only attended three of these assemblies previously!

## Quick Start: Oracy assembly checklist

- Clear objective (oracy focus + content link)
- Entry prompt ready (with stems/vocab)
- Rules refreshed and target skill named
- Oracy Detectives briefed (prompt sheet in hand)
- Stage 1–4 slides (spark → context → apply → celebrate)
- Calm exit routine

# Chapter 8:
## Specific praise

## Strategy description

Pupils learn a lot from the praise they receive. That's why teachers often use proximity praise to reinforce behaviours we want all pupils to adopt.

Webster-Stratton (2007), early adopters of this approach, explains:

*"The quality of the teacher's attention emerges as one of the most important factors in helping students become motivated and successful learners. Consistent and meaningful encouragement and praise from a teacher nurtures and increases children's academic and social competence. Children who are praised are self-confident, have high self-esteem, and seem to internalize these early messages. Over time, giving more praise and positive attention to children for their progress [...] can be beneficial for all the students [...] because these labelled descriptions of the expected academic and social behaviours act as a reminder of expected behaviour for the other children."*

When used consistently to reference oracy behaviours, specific praise can have a strong, positive impact.

## Context

Praise should be everywhere, from everyone. But specific praise doesn't always come naturally. You may need to support and train staff in how to make it explicit.

Think of this as embedding a shared language around oracy across your setting.

## Prior learning required

Specific praise builds directly on the basic, respectful oracy skills (see chapter 2). To maximise its impact, link your praise back to the oracy rules you've already agreed as a school. That way, pupils hear consistent messages about what's valued.

## Useful scaffolds

The only scaffold you really need:

- A poster of your oracy expectations, visible to pupils.

- A cue/reminder for staff (e.g. matching image on your whiteboard or in your teaching notes).

This helps teachers remember to highlight oracy behaviours *in the moment*, and shows pupils what behaviours will be praised.

## Implementation across the age phases

The differences in implementation lie in how pupils understand praise and which rules/behaviours they are familiar with. Below are examples of age-appropriate praise linked to the four strands of oracy.

## Impact

When pupils hear consistent, explicit praise, the language and behaviours become part of their self-expectation and peer culture.

If you repeatedly say, "Thank you for looking at me when I was speaking – it made me feel listened to," pupils will begin to understand that this is valued and praise-worthy behaviour.

The ripple effect will occur when pupils start praising each other specifically. At first, you may scaffold this ("I liked when you…", "Thank you for…"). Over time, they will internalise the habit, distinguishing between *teaching through talk* and *teaching to talk*.

The payoff is lessons where discussion deepens content learning *and* develops oracy – not one at the expense of the other.

EYFS

- "Your friends could hear you beautifully when you said…"
- "Well done for remembering that we do not shout indoors."
- "It was really kind when you said…"
- "___ is such a great word, I am going to try to use that!"
- "I can tell you thought carefully…"
- "Well done for waiting for X to finish speaking."

**KS1**

Oracy in our classroom

**Use a big voice**
Hello!
Speak loud enough for friends to hear.

**Use good words**
Please
Try to use full sentences.
Change your voice to show.

**Think before you speak**
2=
1=
Have a think, then share your idea.
Add detail.
Give reasons or examples.

**Take turns**
Work together.
Respond to what your friends say and build on their ideas.

- "I love how you used…"
- "Your voice tells me you are feeling…"
- "Well done for using a full sentence…"
- "__ is a great word to use because…"
- "Thank you for giving me extra information by saying…"
- "I can tell you thought really carefully about…"
- "I can tell you have listened to X because…"
- "Well done for building onto X's idea by saying…"

| KS2 | |
|---|---|
| **Physical** | |
| • Use a big voice – speak clearly so everyone can hear.<br>• Use pace and tone – change how fast or slow you talk, and adjust your tone to match the situation. | • "I liked how you used a big voice so everyone could hear you."<br>• "You spoke clearly and that helped the whole class understand."<br>• "The way you changed your pace/voice made your idea more interesting."<br>• "I noticed you slowed down to make your message clear – that was very effective." |
| **Linguistic** | |
| • Use good words – choose clever and kind words.<br>• Expand vocabulary – try new words and phrases to make your ideas stronger. | • "I like the kind words you chose when you spoke to your partner."<br>• "You used a really strong/interesting word there, which made your idea even better."<br>• "I noticed you tried a new word in your sentence – well done for being brave with your vocabulary."<br>• "Your full sentence helped everyone follow your idea." |
| **Cognitive** | |
| • Think before you speak – Have a think, then share your idea.<br>• Explain and justify – Give reasons, examples, or evidence to back up what you say. | • "You thought carefully before speaking and that made your idea clear."<br>• "I liked how you explained your idea with a reason/example."<br>• "The detail you gave really helped me understand your thinking."<br>• "You gave evidence to back up your point – that made it stronger." |
| **Social and emotional** | |
| • Take turns – work together and respond to your friends' ideas.<br>• Build discussion – ask questions, agree or disagree politely to keep the conversation going. | • "I liked how you waited for your turn and listened carefully."<br>• "You built on your friend's idea really well."<br>• "You responded politely, and that helped the discussion keep going."<br>• "You worked together by asking a helpful question – that moved the talk forward." |

| KS3 | |
|---|---|
| **Physical** | |
| • Use a big voice – speak clearly so everyone can hear.<br>• Use pace and tone – change how fast or slow you talk, and adjust your tone to match the situation.<br>• Use body language – use gestures, posture and eye contact to strengthen your message. | • "I liked the way you spoke clearly so everyone could hear – your voice carried well."<br>• "You used your tone really effectively to show how important that point was."<br>• "Your eye contact and hand gestures really helped get your message across." |
| **Linguistic** | |
| • Use good words – choose clever and kind words.<br>• Expand vocabulary – try new words and phrases to make your ideas stronger.<br>• Adapt language for audience – select formal or informal words depending on who you are speaking to. | • "You chose such precise words there – it made your idea very clear."<br>• "I noticed you used new vocabulary today. That made your explanation stronger."<br>• "You adapted your language really well for your audience – that was thoughtful and effective." |
| **Cognitive** | |
| • Think before you speak – have a think, then share your idea.<br>• Explain and justify – give reasons, examples or evidence to back up what you say.<br>• Build arguments – link ideas together logically to create clear, persuasive points. | • "You paused before speaking, and it made your point more focused and clear."<br>• "I like how you gave an example to justify your idea – it made your argument convincing."<br>• "The way you linked your points together showed strong reasoning skills." |
| **Social and emotional** | |
| • Take turns – work together and respond to your friends' ideas.<br>• Build discussion – ask questions, agree, or disagree politely to keep the conversation going.<br>• Lead and facilitate – guide group talk by including others and managing the discussion. | • "You waited for your turn and responded politely – that kept the discussion flowing."<br>• "You built on your partner's idea really thoughtfully, which moved the conversation forward."<br>• "You helped include others in the discussion – that showed real leadership." |

| Dining Room | |
|---|---|
| **Physical** | |
| • KS1: Use a big voice but not a shout, so your friends can hear you at the table.<br>• KS2: Use a clear, calm voice that matches the busy dining room – speak so others nearby can join in. | • "I like the way you're using a big voice without shouting – that makes it easy for your friends to hear you."<br>• "You spoke so clearly just then. Everyone at your table could understand you."<br>• "You kept your voice calm even though it's busy in here – well done." |
| **Linguistic** | |
| • KS1: Use kind words like "please" and "thank you."<br>• KS2: Choose polite and respectful words when asking or offering things at the table. | • "I noticed you said 'please/thank you' – that was very polite."<br>• "Great job using such kind words when you asked for help."<br>• "I like how you used clear words to explain what you wanted – it made things easier." |
| **Cognitive** | |
| • KS1: Think before you speak – wait until you've swallowed before talking.<br>• KS2: Share ideas and stories while you eat, and explain them clearly so everyone understands. | • "You waited until you finished chewing before speaking – that showed good thinking and good manners."<br>• "I liked how you shared a story so clearly that your friends could follow along."<br>• "You gave a really good example in your story – that made it even more interesting." |
| **Social and emotional** | |
| • KS1: Take turns – listen when your friends are talking.<br>• KS2: Join in conversations by asking questions and including others at the table. | • "I like the way you listened carefully while your friend was talking."<br>• "You included everyone at your table by asking them a question – that was kind."<br>• "You built on your friend's idea really well – that kept the conversation going." |

## Top Tip: CELEBRATE!

Make oracy praise visible and valued.

One of my favourite strategies to celebrate oracy was with a class that enjoyed having a weekly Oracy Star.
This teacher had an award shaped like a microphone and that pupil was allowed to keep the award in front of them on their desk for the entire week!

# Oracy Star of the Week!

Awarded to

_____

Date: _____

An easy way to celebrate oracy on a whole school level is to include it in your celebration assemblies. There could be an Oracy Class of the Week or each class could highlight their Oracy Star.
Staff would need to provide a specific reason which links to the four strands of oracy for why that pupil or class have been awarded.

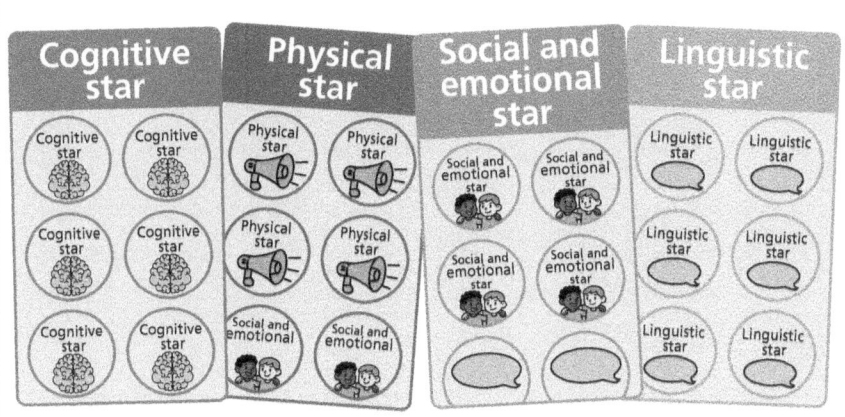

One lovely oracy centred school had specific stickers designed and printed for their pupils. This was really special because it was obvious what the pupil had done well in and others were able to celebrate this too.

This also brought the parents into the conversation more often than if their child randomly received a certificate.

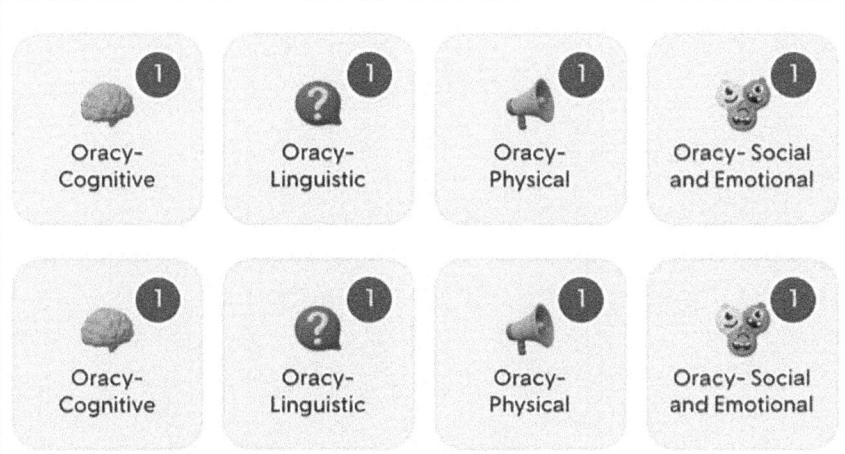

*ClassDojo – Online Classroom Management Platform*

If you use an online platform to award points or similar system try to organise this so praise is explicit when added.

This allows pupils to know what they are doing well in and also gives you an overview of where class and pupil strengths lie and where gaps may be in oracy abilities.

# Chapter 9: Maths

## Strategy description

There isn't just one neat strategy for oracy in maths. Instead, it's about spotting the opportunities (and there are *so many*) and then harnessing them. Maths is absolutely a place for oracy – but not everyone sees it that way.

## Context

I've noticed that oracy and maths are almost the Marmite of the oracy world, although it's not about whether teachers like it or not – it's about whether they can *see* it. For some, it's obvious. Of course, maths is talk-rich, of course it relies on reasoning and explanation. For others, the link feels invisible: "I can't see how it fits at all."

This chapter is mainly for those who can't see it yet. However, if you're already embracing oracy in maths, you might still find some extra sparks here.

One of the best CPD sessions I've ever attended was *Maths – No Problem!* with the incredible Dr Yeap Ban Har, a leading figure in Singapore Maths. The whole day was inspirational, but one line has stuck with me ever since:

*"A quiet classroom is a suspicious classroom."*

I couldn't agree more. The best maths learning happens through collaborative discussion, carefully scaffolded for both oracy and maths. And it's not just about partner talk – the class also needs space to share back together, so everyone hears more than just their partner's perspective.

Talk is where misconceptions surface. It's where children try out their reasoning, where ideas bump against each other and where we as teachers can step in to repair and guide. Maths now places so much emphasis on reasoning that we *have* to give children the skills to explain the *how* and the *why*. Oracy is the most powerful way to do that.

## Prior learning required

As with everything in this book, pupils need to start with the basic, respectful oracy rules. They need to know how to listen, how to take turns, how to respect each other's ideas. Those rules need to be revisited constantly, tied into praise and explicitly modelled with a running commentary so pupils can see what good oracy looks like in practice.

## My own experience

I've always leaned on the CPA approach – concrete, pictorial, abstract. I love the buzz of a classroom where pupils are getting hands-on, manipulating counters, drawing diagrams and then moving to symbols. But if I think back to my early career, those lessons were often chaotic. Counters everywhere, children "exploring" without really moving forward and me trying to keep a lid on it all!

I'm not alone. A colleague once summed it up perfectly for me:

*"The big light bulb for me was when those discussions and those collaborative things worked so much better because I'd actually consciously set them up properly for the first time … You're going to have talk in your classroom anyway, so why not just do it really well?"*

After my Singapore Maths training, I realised what had been missing. The structure. The scaffolds. Once those were in place, the chaos melted away and the conversations had real depth.

Another colleague put it beautifully:

*"Maths was transformed for me when children had to explain their reasoning. It flipped the teaching – suddenly they were doing the work, not me. Their understanding shot up because they were thinking and talking, not just copying."*

The difference is stark: manipulatives on their own can lead to chaos. Manipulatives with oracy scaffolds lead to mastery.

And this isn't just my view. Rupert Knight, now a university lecturer, described to me the same turning point (though in science lessons back in the 1990s).

- He started giving children roles (summariser, questioner, challenger).

- Group work suddenly became purposeful.

- Pupils who struggled with writing could shine through spoken roles.

The principle is the same in maths as all other areas: the set-up matters. If you structure the talk, the learning follows.

## Implementation

Here are a few of the ways I've seen oracy transform maths:

- **Sentence stems**
  These are gold dust. "I know this because…", "Another way we could…", "I can prove it by…". These give children the confidence and language to reason.

- **Target vocabulary**
  Putting the right words on the board focuses the talk. It also gives you a quick AfL snapshot of who really understands.

- **Stem sentence slides**
  Pop your sentence stems into your slides so they're visible prompts. It stops talk drifting and keeps children aiming high.

- **The "prove it" question**
  One of the most powerful prompts you can give. Even better when children start saying it to each other "Can you prove that?"

## Useful scaffolds

The scaffolds aren't anything new – they're the same ones you'll have seen throughout this book: rules, roles, stems, vocabulary prompts. The difference in maths is that they sit alongside manipulatives. Oracy and equipment, side by side.

## Implementation across the age phases

I often hear: "Oracy in maths? That's fine for younger children, but it's not relevant higher up." I couldn't disagree more.

Here's one of my favourite stories.

I was in a school staffroom when a Year 6 teacher looked me dead in the eye and said: "Don't bother coming into my maths lesson – you won't see any oracy. We're doing SATs prep." I smiled, nodded, and asked what they were working on. She explained the class were stuck on one area of the practice papers, and she was having to unpick it heavily for them.

So I shared an idea I'd seen in a secondary classroom.

- Pupils look at a practice question on their own first, jotting initial thoughts.
- They pair up and share ideas.
- Pairs join another pair, and the four have to reach consensus on the best method, and why they believe this.
- Groups share back while the teacher notes repeated vocabulary and common strategies.

The magic? By the time pupils worked independently again, they had not only the strategies but also the language to explain them.

At lunchtime that same teacher came back to me smiling: "That was the best maths lesson I've taught in ages. The children finally got it."

That's the power of oracy – sometimes all it takes is a different approach.

## Impact

Maths assessment now leans heavily on reasoning. If we don't build in oracy, we're effectively holding pupils back.

But more than that: if children can't *say* it, they haven't truly learned it. Talking through methods, explaining reasoning, proving answers – these are what secure maths learning in long-term memory.

And don't forget: children learn the most when teaching others. Oracy in maths makes that possible.

# Chapter 10:
## Boss and Assistant

## Strategy description

Imagine standing in an office dictating a letter to an assistant who types as you speak. Boss and Assistant replicates that dynamic in the classroom: two pupils, two roles, one giving clear step-by-step instructions while the other executes them.

## Context

This is brilliant in maths (procedures, multi-step problems), but it transfers well to computing, DT, science investigations, geography fieldwork methods or even writing (planning instructions, algorithms, or lab reports). Explore widely!

## Prior learning required

- Class oracy rules (listening, body language, turn-taking, voice levels).
- Respectful back-and-forth (don't speak over; ask, don't bark).
- Basic instructional language (first, next, then, because…).
- How to answer a question politely and precisely.

## Implementation

The idea behind Boss and Assistant is that the Boss instructs the assistant on what to do, step by step, clearly. The Boss is **not** allowed to join in the practicality of the activity. They can only direct. The Assistant's role is to follow the instructions. However, they are encouraged to question their boss. We want to encourage children to not just accept what they are told by authority figures but to question when they are unsure or disagree. They may want to ask why their Boss has chosen a certain approach or if their Boss is sure that is the correct step to take. They may also ask the important question of "Why?". "Can you tell me why you are choosing to do that?" "Can you tell me why you have chosen to do this that way?" When modelling to the pupils ensure the Assistant demonstrates this.

**Boss and Assistant steps**

After teaching the main learning:

1. Model with a pupil (or a supporting adult). Make roles explicit.

   - Boss: gives only verbal instructions. No touching the equipment/whiteboard.

   - Assistant: follows each instruction exactly but can question for clarity/accuracy.

2. Coach productive questioning from the Assistant (and model it).

   - "Can you tell me why you're choosing that step?"

   - "Are you sure that comes next?"

   - "Could you rephrase that so I know what to draw/move/write?"

   - "What does this number represent in the expression?"

3. Run in pairs, then swap roles. Circulate, listening for misconceptions and noting great phrasing to share.

## Metacognitive moment

When you model, think aloud as Boss and invite the Assistant to challenge you. You're teaching how to explain, justify and refine.

# Useful scaffolds

- Visible prompt list for the Assistant's questions.

- Target vocabulary bank for the lesson (e.g. "divide", "groups", "remainder", "algorithm", "loop", "variable").

- Your oracy rules displayed where all can see.

- One whiteboard and pen per pair to force turn-taking.

## My own experience

As an EYFS/KS1 specialist, I'd mostly parked this – until a Year 2 division lesson on balancing simple expressions. Initially, confident pupils led while others followed. I reset: one whiteboard per pair, introduced Boss and Assistant, and modelled:

- Boss dictated the expression.
- Boss explained what each number represents.
- Assistant drew groups and shared items, querying each step.
- Roles were swapped.

Engagement in the room skyrocketed, questioning improved, a lower-attaining, under-confident pair modelled perfectly. It was the best maths lesson I'd taught in a while!

### Top Tips

- **Pull it together publicly** End with a quick pupil demo. Behind the presenters, display target vocabulary. Ask listeners to track usage and be ready to give feedback ("Which key words did they use accurately?"). Remember – all pupils engaged at all times!

- **Carpet Detectives** Assign the listening children to all become detectives. Give them a clear focus to observe and explain that one pupil will be selected at random to feed back.

## Strategies to embed these skills

- **EAL / Vocabulary gaps** Add visuals of each step and a mini word bank. Allow the Assistant to point to images.

- **Confidence** Start with very small steps and tightly scaffolded stems. Let the more hesitant pupil be Assistant first.

- **Misconceptions** Use a worked example alongside to anchor correctness. Pause and re-model a single tricky step.

- **Selective mutism / speech and language needs** As an alternative to pairs you could run trios (Boss, Assistant, Evaluator). The Evaluator could track steps and key vocabulary and can read aloud agreed sentence stems. The pupil with selective mutism can still participate through drawing, pointing or using story maps. Over time, with practice in the Assistant role, pupils often begin to find comfortable ways to communicate. At this point they may start to experiment with being the Boss, perhaps giving instructions through the use of writing, stock images or their own diagrams. Pupils are fascinating in the ways they find to communicate and how they come to understand one another.

It comes down to your creativity when approaching adaptations to include and involve all pupils, ensuring high levels of engagement at all times.

## Implementation across the age phases

| EYFS | Simple imparting of instructions. "Tell your partner to...", or "Listen to your partner and do what they say..." |
|---|---|
| KS1 | One partner instructing others to do something. Partner listening and following the instructions without ad-libbing. Encourage pupils asking simple questions when they think their partner has made a mistake. |
| KS2 | One pupil instructing a partner or small group. Expectation of Assistant questioning potential errors. Vocabulary bank on offer to encourage a higher level of language. Pupils begin to evaluate Boss's speech. "Could you improve how you said that?" "Instead of saying X, could you..." |
| KS3 and above | Carry out activity in trios, one Boss, one Assistant and one pupil evaluating. Vocabulary could be placed into a bullseye allowing the Evaluator to total a number of points based on the language used. Assistant still able to question and aid up levelled language. Evaluator could reward any errors or misconceptions Assistant highlights in a constructive way. |

## Impact

- You hear pupils' procedural understanding live and catch misconceptions early.

- Passive learners become active: everyone explains or executes.

- The structure doubles as retrieval practice, strengthening schemas in long-term memory.

- Pupil language shifts from *doing* to explaining and justifying – lifting both oracy and subject outcomes.

# Chapter 11:
## Oracy CPD

## Strategy description

The crux of getting your whole staff to buy in:

- What will you deliver to staff?
- How will you do this?
- How will you plan what your CPD will look like?

## Context

Your approach to CPD will make or break oracy implementation.

- Some oracy leads are given the role with little more than: "Oh, you can be oracy lead." Don't panic – this is common. Many of the most successful oracy leads began this way, growing their knowledge alongside their school's practice.

- Others begin in schools where SLT have already invested time, resources and energy into oracy. That provides a stronger start, but the journey is still long.

Wherever you begin, remember: oracy implementation is not a quick win, but a whole-school journey. Success rests on the quality, relevance and consistency of your CPD offer.

## Prior learning required

Oracy must align with whole-school priorities. If your school is already mid-way through a major improvement drive (e.g. a new phonics scheme), it may not be the right time to launch oracy school-wide.

But this doesn't stop individual teachers, year groups or departments from exploring oracy strategies in their own classrooms. Drip-feeding ideas this way builds confidence, readiness and future champions.

## Implementation

Oracy journeys look different in every school – just as children develop at different rates. Priorities, demographics and contexts mean no two schools will follow the same path.

To illustrate, I've created example road maps of three schools (see Figure 11.1):

- One with very high EAL and pupil mobility.
- One with high pupil premium intake.
- One in a more affluent setting.

Despite their differences, each journey lasted at least two years – most longer. The best oracy practitioners view this as a pedagogical stance, not a tick-box scheme. There is always another refinement to make, another strategy to embed. Oracy is not a target to reach but a practice that grows, adapts and strengthens over time.

## My own experience

The best CPD is immersive. Sitting through a PowerPoint rarely shifts practice. Experiencing oracy as a learner does.

- In my CPD, staff take part in the strategies as if they were pupils.
- Resources are handed out, activities are modelled, teachers practise.
- This immediacy makes translation to the classroom more natural, as staff have had the time to visualise.

These are the teachers who, the following week, pop into my classroom to share a success: "I tried that sentence stem activity, and it worked!" The lightbulb moments come not from me *telling*, but from staff *doing*.

## Strategies to embed these skills

Not everyone will jump on board. Some staff are comfortable and don't want to change long-established routines.

Time is another barrier – both timetable time for whole-staff CPD and staff goodwill for extras.

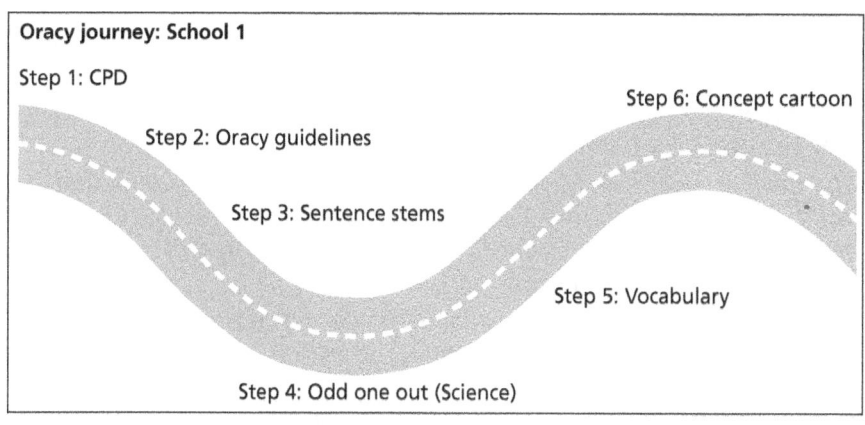

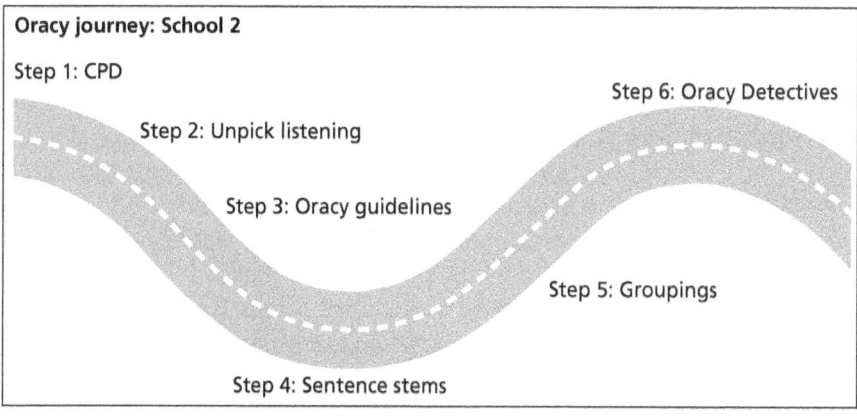

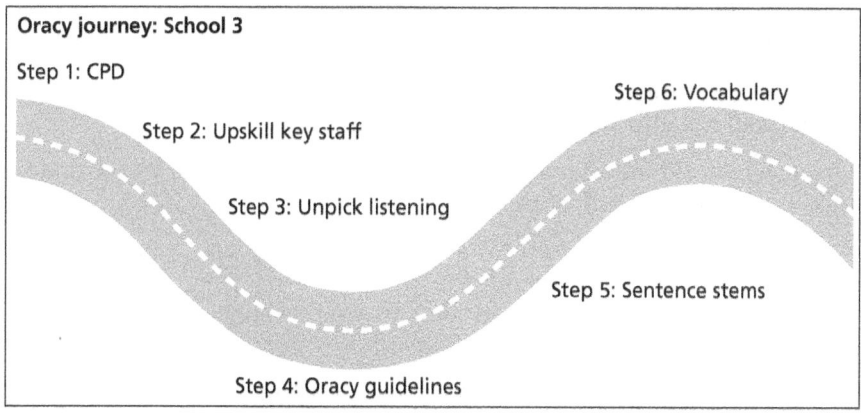

Figure 11.1 Example road maps

Paul, the English lead for a multi-academy trust, and a secondary English and oracy specialist:

*"I found my initial training failed because I delivered it as 'here's the strategy, now you can do it.' It didn't stick.*

*The turning point was when colleagues came into my classroom and saw oracy in action. A history teacher observed a Harkness discussion [see below], loved it and began using it. Soon she was running CPD for her team. Geography colleagues followed.*

*What snowballed was organic, subject-specific experimentation. Staff even started emailing: 'I'm trying this strategy in period 3 – come and watch if you're free.'*

*Oracy spread not because I demanded it, but because teachers saw its impact, shared their successes, and generated their own buzz."*

The Harkness discussion model originated in the 1930s, developed by Edward Harkness. It is a strategy widely used by oracy educators. In its simplest form, the group discussion is tracked as it unfolds. This is valuable from several assessment-focused viewpoints, both for the teacher and for the pupil summarising the conversation. For the teacher, it provides a clear picture of which pupils participated, who contributed most frequently and who spoke less or not at all. You might also jot additional notes, such as vocabulary used or the type of contribution made – building on ideas,

## Impact

We've all sat through the CPD that makes us think: "I will never get this time back." Equally, we've left CPD buzzing with ideas.

One teacher told me after a twilight: "I love your CPD – all I have to do is talk! I don't find it hard work."

At first, I worried this meant my sessions lacked rigour. Then I reframed: staff were engaged, accountable and applying what they practised. That teacher, in fact, was one of the first to trial strategies with Reception children and return to share her success.

If adults can leave CPD feeling relaxed, confident and motivated to try something new, imagine the effect when pupils feel the same about oracy rich lessons.

# Chapter 12:
## Oracy leadership

*"Do not run before you can walk."*
*Exact quote given by every contributor interviewed.*

## Strategy description

Oracy leadership is huge. Until you begin the journey and really grasp what oracy is, you can't appreciate its all-encompassing nature.

This chapter is for anyone who has ever felt overwhelmed by the scale of leading oracy. Think of it as a map, and a reminder that this is not a sprint but a marathon.

## My own experience

Throughout my oracy journey, I've surrounded myself with like-minded, passionate teachers. I've worked within strong oracy teams, school working parties, local networks, Multi-Academy Trusts and alongside national charities.

What I've learned is that oracy has a devoted, supportive community. Without my network, I wouldn't be the oracy champion I am today. These colleagues kept my curiosity alive and helped me stay motivated – and I hope I've done the same for them.

I drew on their wisdom to shape this book. When I reviewed my research notes and conversations, four clear takeaways emerged.

# Colleague insight: Steven's oracy journey

In his second year of teaching, Steven found himself delivering assemblies written for KS2 pupils to KS1 children. He knew they were pitched wrong but didn't yet feel confident enough to adapt them.

The turning point came when he remembered an oracy-rich assembly from a placement. Instead of standing at the front for 20 minutes, he let the children work in groups and talk. The difference was instant: children were engaged, learning and actually enjoying assembly.

Moving to an infant school, Steven and his year group partner (the school's oracy lead) began embedding oracy into daily practice. They started with the Listening Ladder (see chapter 3) to teach explicit listening skills, then introduced their own Talk Tactics as whole-school oracy rules.

| | | |
|---|---|---|
| **I sit …** | in my space. | |
| | calmly. | |
| | facing the speaker. | |
| **I listen …** | carefully so I understand. | |
| | and react to what has been said. | |
| **I talk …** | when it is my turn. | |
| | at an appropriate volume. | |
| | in full sentences. | |
| **I can …** | build on an idea. | |
| | challenge an idea politely. | |

Figure 12.1 The Talk Tactics Steven created and uses at his school as oracy rules for all children.

To capture understanding, Steven trialled QR codes. Children recorded spoken explanations rather than struggling to write everything down. The depth of reasoning was far richer, and retention improved dramatically.

Over time, colleagues saw the impact for themselves: oracy wasn't just about talk – it was raising engagement, strengthening behaviour, and even lifting writing outcomes.

## Vision, purpose and priorities

Use your school priorities to be absolutely clear on your purpose. Establish how oracy will help you to achieve this purpose. Oracy is not a tick-box exercise – you are aiming to create and share a meaningful, tried and tested pedagogy. As a leader you must continually reflect on how oracy is enriching and impacting learning. You need to be sure that pupils are engaged in genuine cognitive processes rather than parroting what they have heard. Are you hearing genuine pupil voices or teachers' repeated words? As a whole school you must have clarity on what high-quality oracy looks like in your context and the steps pupils and staff need to take to achieve this.

**Takeaway #1: Oracy must serve a clear purpose and be rooted in your school's vision.**

## Leadership and whole-school culture

For oracy to really thrive, it must hold status across the school and community where possible. This means including it in CPD, performance management and curriculum planning so it is valued as a whole-school priority. Establishing a shared language helps everyone work towards the same goal, fostering an "oracy buzz" that builds enthusiasm.

Remember that staff buy-in is essential. Leaders should actively listen to colleagues' reflections, offering staff opportunities for collaboration rather than always working in isolation. Frequent and purposeful, immersive training sessions and strategies to increase staff confidence are key, always remembering that change must be gradual to become sustainable. Over time, as oracy becomes routine, it should naturally weave itself into every area of school life.

**Takeaway #2: Culture change is slow – but lasting when shared.**

## Teacher development and CPD

It is important that teachers still see themselves as learners. They should be open to engaging in inquiry and reflection to improve their practice. When you allow teachers the space to start small in safe contexts their confidence will grow organically. During this period ensure that practice is shared through open classrooms and peer discussions. This will help to develop and grow a collaborative colleague culture. Up-to-date research should guide growth and direction, and all CPD should be used purposefully to strengthen knowledge and confidence.

It is very powerful when leaders model any desired behaviours, language and strategies. I live by the mantra that I would never ask anyone to do something I would not do myself. I will mop up sick, make coffee and back boards. If I am asking teachers to try new things I will only ever do this if I have explored it myself first. This means it is already part of my mental model and I can use this knowledge to help others.

As a leader you need to be aware of staff strengths while also supporting areas for development. Be creative with the opportunities for oracy. Use low-pressure environments for staff to trial oracy approaches and build up their individual experience, consider using themed days or special events, when timetables and content coverage are less time constrained.

**Takeaway #3: Model first. Let teachers learn by doing, not just hearing.**

## Implementation and monitoring

As I mentioned above, oracy implementation should be steady, deliberate and always linked to school priorities. Frequent and specific monitoring will ensure that pupils' oracy skills are transferable and consistently applied across the curriculum. School leaders should avoid rushing implementation and instead see the value in breaking the process into manageable steps. Please recognise and appreciate that pedagogical change takes time. Persistence and enthusiasm are essential. Oracy is not an add-on, but a teaching approach and this requires slowly and carefully embedding into daily practice within school. Bear in mind that gradual, well-paced, change leads to sustainable improvements and long-lasting impact.

**Takeaway #4: Oracy isn't an add-on. It's a teaching approach – and embedding it takes patience.**

## Strategies to embed these skills

The big question at every training: "What about the hard-to-reach staff who just won't buy in?"

Sadly, to this I don't have a magic answer. What I've found is that being personable, collaborative and honest makes the biggest difference. Don't tell – do. Demonstration beats direction every time.

# Chapter 13:
## Final thoughts from my contributors

## Hannah 1

*Primary teacher and key stage leader*

### Hannah's oracy go-to

For Hannah, a vocabulary-first sequence that starts with a visual prompt (images), then explicit vocabulary, then the facts/input is her go-to. She also plans with tiered vocab in mind and uses stems to encourage pupils to use full sentences.

*"What do you think is happening in the images … now I'm going to give you the vocabulary … now I'm going to give you the facts … it's transformed the learning in my classroom this year."*

### Hannah's barrier to oracy implementation

Time and whole-school consistency – competing priorities, staffing turbulence, and slipping buy-in (people default to reusing old plans).

*"The buzz has dropped off … because I'm not given the time for it." "We're stuck in a bit of a cycle of 'we did this last year so we'll reuse the plan'."*

### Hannah's Top Tip

Pick one focus and do it well (e.g. listening ladder or vocab-led stems). Use explicit, in-the-moment teaching, model and insist on full sentences/target vocab, and be patient–change is gradual.

*"Pick the thing that you want to focus on … do it in small steps and do it well." "The most effective oracy teaching … is that explicit teaching in the moment." "You're not going to crack it in a week."*

# Steven

*Infant school teacher and curriculum lead*

### Steven's oracy go-to

Steven uses a four-part approach: Talk Tactics (adapted into simple, infant-friendly guidelines), Talk Detectives to monitor talk quality, Trios (instead of pairs, to scaffold for EAL/new pupils) and sentence stems to get children started and then gradually fade.

*"When they speak, the reasoning is richer than the sentence they would struggle to write."*

### Steven's barrier to oracy implementation

The biggest challenge is consistency and patience. Teachers sometimes see oracy as a one-off lesson, or resist changing long-held habits. Sustained embedding takes time, persistence, and careful scaffolding.

*"If it's just a one-off lesson ... it's not really going to work. It needs to be consistent, it's not a standalone subject – it needs to be throughout the curriculum."*

### Steven's Top Tip

Start with listening – break it down explicitly and treat it as a skill to be taught, not assumed. Be patient, scaffold heavily at first, model relentlessly and expand step by step across classes and year groups.

*"Start with listening first ... don't expect it to be quick. Be patient. You've got to be enthusiastic and model it, even at ten to three on a wet Tuesday – because children are impressionable."*

# Alice

*Primary school teacher and oracy lead*

### Alice's oracy go-to

Mixed-ability trios as the default grouping (one can model, one can try, one can listen/learn). Quick, plug-and-play talk games (e.g. Odd One Out) and a bank of blank concept-cartoon templates she can edit on the fly. Visible talk guidelines (her infant-friendly version of Talk Tactics).

*"If you've got a sentence stem on the board, a talk trio and your talk guidelines up, most of your lesson will work."*

### Alice's barrier to oracy implementation

Staff equating "It's time to talk" with oracy – no modelling, no sentence stems, no listening instruction. Implementation drag in a MAT where priorities shift with trends.

*"People think just giving children opportunities to talk is oracy. It isn't – without modelling and scaffolds they can't do it."*

### Alice's Top Tip

Start tiny, drip-feed, and build a culture, not a compliance checklist. Go and see oracy in action at a school that's doing it – seeing beats reading!

*"Don't be worried – it's massive. Focus on one small thing, embed it, then move to the next. And go and see it being done.*

# Jaz

*School improvement lead for a multi-academy trust*

### Jaz's oracy go-to

For Jaz, the go-to isn't a single classroom trick – it's embedding oracy right into the curriculum design and making articulation the non-negotiable golden thread. She frames it simply: if children can't articulate their learning, they can't access the curriculum.

*"We can give them the progression maps, the vocabulary, the nuggets of information ... but if they haven't got the words or the sentences to articulate it, how are you going to do that?"*

### Jaz's barrier to oracy implementation

The main barrier Jaz identifies is leadership buy-in. In her experience, oracy cannot survive as a side initiative or a personal passion project. It has to be embedded in school development plans, linked to performance management and championed from the very top.

*"If the headteacher is not interested, just save yourself the time and energy because it's not going to happen. It falls by the wayside unless it's whole school."*

### Jaz's Top Tip

Her advice for anyone starting out: be clear on *why* you want oracy in your school, and do the research to make that case. Don't jump straight to activities or schemes until you've defined your purpose.

*"First ask: what does oracy mean to you, and what do you want the impact to be? If you can't answer that, it won't work. Do the research. Know your pitch. Then the journey will look different depending on your context."*

# Paul

*English lead for a multi-academy trust, secondary English and oracy specialist*

### Paul's oracy go-to

Harkness discussions: he sees them as the fastest way to surface depth, comparison and synthesis (especially for literature and unseen poetry), and as a gateway that gets sceptical colleagues hooked once they *see* it working.

*"People think Harkness is 'advanced', but it was the first thing I tried and it's the most powerful when it's scaffolded well."*

### Paul's barrier to oracy implementation

Time and confidence – after-hours "now go and do it" CPD flopped. Curriculum leads wouldn't surrender the extra time and many teachers were nervous about letting go. What changed things was live modelling and targeted invites to come and watch oracy in action.

*"I did training and went, 'OK, now you can do it.' It just didn't work ... until colleagues saw it in a real lesson."*

### Paul's Top Tip

Add clear parameters to talk and start with one trusted class. Build momentum by showcasing wins (students speaking for themselves helps), then balance organic growth with a few smart non-negotiables (e.g. a Harkness slot in Y7, a no-pens day, a speech unit). Pick willing departments and champions first. Spread by invitation and example.

*"Open talk isn't enough – set the stems, the vocabulary, the stimulus. Those guardrails get students to the end point you want."*

# Hannah 2

*Education consultant for Leicester City Local Authority*

### Hannah's oracy go-to

Taking your words for a walk – adapted from drama training. Pupils walk around, voice chosen lines or drafts aloud, then share with whoever they meet. It gives freedom, confidence and a safe way to rehearse ideas before committing them to paper.

*"It let them hear their own voices before it mattered what they were saying."*

### Hannah's barrier to oracy implementation

Teachers sometimes treat oracy as "just let them talk" without scaffolds or purpose. The real pitfall is not understanding *why* a strategy is being used – then it falls flat (like traverses without a good prompt). Adults can be the same: overloaded in CPD, expected to "just get on with it" without step-by-step practice.

*"If you haven't thought about why you're using a strategy, it won't work – for children or for staff."*

### Hannah's Top Tip

Start small, with purpose. Be clear on what you want and why, have enough subject knowledge to scaffold it properly. Create networks and collaborative spaces where teachers experience strategies themselves, reflect and share how they'll use them. Build step by step – don't overload.

*"Never underestimate what children are capable of – but you've got to know how to get it from them."*

# Rupert

*Associate professor in education, teaches on Primary ITE courses and other postgraduate courses*

### Rupert's oracy go-to

Rupert always falls back on structured opportunities for everyone to speak, most often Think–Pair–Share (or Trios). He stresses that giving proper wait time and eavesdropping on talk allows him to assess learning and build a richer whole-class discussion without dominating it himself.

*"Those little Think–Pair–Share moments are easy wins – they give everyone a voice, they let me eavesdrop, and they stop me taking over the discussion."*

### Rupert's barrier to oracy implementation

He sees the biggest barrier as teachers' anxiety about letting go of control. Noise levels, unpredictable content and the fear of a senior leader walking in can all push teachers back towards safe, teacher-led routines.

*"The danger is you see the noise or uncertainty as a pitfall and then think, well I just won't do it. Instead, you've got to learn how to do it properly."*

### Rupert's Top Tip

His advice is to be clear on your purpose and start small: pick one or two routines and do them consistently well before layering in more. And, importantly, keep a learner's mindset yourself.

*"Don't try and do everything – teach yourself and your class a couple of strategies you can use across the curriculum, and do those really well."*

## Ali

*Primary headteacher*

### Ali's oracy go-to

As a headteacher, Ali's go-to isn't a single classroom trick but the whole-school culture of giving children a voice. She sees oracy as the best way to improve learning across the curriculum and to prepare pupils for life beyond school – academically, socially and emotionally.

*"For us, children having a voice will enable them to succeed in life in the wider world … we want our children to be taken seriously."*

### Ali's barrier to oracy implementation

Ali acknowledges that staffing changes and finding time were potential barriers. Initially, she worried about getting new staff up to speed, but the team's enthusiasm quickly turned the challenge into a strength. Beyond logistics, she hasn't faced resistance – parents, governors, staff and pupils have all been strongly supportive.

*"That barrier became a positive – the new staff have excelled in everything we've asked them to do, and more."*

### Ali's Top Tip

Her advice is to be ambitious and believe in children's capacity to rise to high expectations. Oracy empowers all learners, including EAL and SEN pupils, by boosting confidence, vocabulary and self-esteem.

*"Raise those expectations – don't put a ceiling on their learning. Oracy shows they can do it."*

## Jass and Hiza

*Primary teachers*

### Jass and Hiza's oracy go-to

Their classroom go-to is using the word jar and rich vocabulary prompts as a springboard for talk. They slow lessons down, deliberately unpick texts and concepts and give pupils the space to talk, think and revisit words again and again until they stick.

*"We'll spend two days on a page of text – pulling it apart, questioning, verbalising – and the children are amazed by the language they discover."*

### Jass and Hiza's barrier to oracy implementation

The main barrier is external pressure for written evidence. Too often teachers feel accountable for filling books rather than building talk. Their school's leadership has been vital in clearing that obstacle, giving permission for talk-first lessons where children's voices are the evidence.

*"Unless schools say, 'It's okay not to have work in the books,' teachers won't feel free to let children talk."*

### Jass and Hiza's Top Tip

Create consistency and safety through repetition. When children know the routines, expectations and sentence stems, even quieter voices join in with confidence. Build a culture where children's spoken contributions are the evidence of learning.

*"The child is your evidence – what they come out with is what's most important."*

# Chapter 14:
## Wider life lessons

As I was putting this book together there were common themes that were coming out that were oracy-orientated but also just great life lessons. I didn't want these to slip past because, as much as we rightly place an importance on an oracy-rich education for attainment and academic success, I believe the real reason we do this work goes deeper. Oracy is about the kind of people our children will become. It is about how they will treat others, how they will listen, how they will stand up for themselves and how they will use their voices in the wider world.

## 1. Communication is humanity's equaliser

Human understanding is fragile when language isn't shared. Often misunderstandings in life – at work, at home, at school – frequently come down to vocabulary and shared meaning. It is vital we teach individuals how to connect clearly and respectfully.

## 2. Respectful listening is as important as speaking

Oracy isn't only about "talking well" – it is about listening with intention, showing kindness and taking turns. This is a life lesson for all individuals – adults as much as children. Meetings, family conversations, even arguments could be transformed if people practised basic, respectful oracy skills.

## 3. Scaffolds don't limit voices, they support voices

Scaffolds do not need to be restrictive. Sentence stems, visuals, and conversational "roles" can actually *open up* children's ability to think, reason and explain. This is applicable to adult life too – frameworks in communication or leadership don't stifle – they give people confidence.

## 4. Change is slow, but it's worth it

Remember that lasting change in schools (and in any organisation) is a long-term process. It takes patience, modelling, consistency and persistence.

## 5. Never underestimate what people are capable of

Passive pupils can suddenly shine when given a scaffold and EAL learners thrive when vocabulary is taught explicitly. Don't write anyone off, ever.

## 6. Joy fuels learning

Whether it's a vocabulary jar, a maths "prove it" question or a child acting out "pounce", there's a thread of joy running through oracy. It's playful, curious and human. Children learn when they feel happy and safe.

## 7. Questioning authority is healthy, not rude

We don't want children to blindly accept what they're told just because it comes from an adult or authority figure. They need to feel safe asking "Why have you chosen to do it this way?" or "Are you sure that's the right step?" That skill doesn't just serve them in school – one day they'll use it with a boss, a colleague or even policymakers. Respectful questioning is how things can improve for all.

## 8. Agreeing and disagreeing respectfully is a life skill

Through shared oracy language, children learn that every space – classrooms, staffrooms, family tables – is full of different opinions. What matters isn't whether we all agree, but whether we can disagree respectfully. Oracy teaches pupils to hold their ground without hostility, and to listen without dismissing or interrupting.

## 9. Respectful communication takes teaching

It's easy to assume children "just know" how to communicate respectfully, but they need exposure to good models, explicit guidance, plenty of practice and constructive feedback. The same is true for adults, if we're honest – respectful communication doesn't come naturally, it's something we learn, rehearse and refine across our whole lives.

# Appendix:
# Definitions

## Cognitive load theory

The idea that working memory is limited and that overloading it can have a negative impact on learning, and that instruction should be designed to take this into account.

Cognitive load theory, first researched by Sweller (1998) towards the late 1980s, is based around the idea that our **working memory** – the part of our mind that processes what we are currently doing – can only deal with a limited amount of information at one time. Reif's (2010) description of cognitive load is extremely useful: "The cognitive load involved in a task is the cognitive effort (or amount of information processing) required by a person to perform this task."

Cognitive load theory suggests that if the cognitive load exceeds our processing capacity, we will struggle to complete the activity successfully. Working memory should be seen as short term and finite, whereas long-term memory can be seen as infinite. The aim should be to move knowledge to long-term memory because when a student is exposed to new material, they can draw on this previous knowledge and the cognitive load is reduced.

## Long-term memory

The mind's storehouse for factual knowledge as well as procedural memory (how to do things). It's not easy to get information into long-term memory, but once there it will likely stick around, potentially forever.

## Schemas and mental models

When we talk about children building schemas or mental models, what we really mean is that they're making sense of the world by connecting new learning to what's already in their heads. Every time pupils meet an idea, word or knowledge again, they're strengthening that schema, making it easier to retrieve and apply in new contexts. Children don't just need to *hear* a word or idea once, they need multiple, meaningful encounters. That's how they form a strong mental model. It's why we keep revisiting, rehearsing and applying vocabulary and concepts – without that repetition, the schema simply won't stick.

You can liken schemas to Velcro strips. At first, there's just a small patch, so only one or two things will cling to it. But each time we revisit, we add more hooks. Soon that strip is strong enough to catch and hold new knowledge easily. That's when children aren't just remembering facts, but actually thinking *with* them.

## Working memory

The mental space in which you briefly hold information that also serves as the staging ground of thought. Working memory is usually thought of as synonymous with consciousness, and its space is limited. Overwhelming working memory is a common reason people get confused.

# References

Department for Children, Schools and Families. (2008). *Personalised learning: A practical guide*. DCSF Publications.

Department for Education. (2014). *National curriculum*. Available at: https://www.gov.uk/government/collections/national-curriculum

Lee, D. and Hatesohl, D. (1983). 'Listening : our most used communication skill'. University of Missouri–Columbia. Available at: https://mospace. umsystem.edu/server/api/core/bitstreams/a2a0746a-e9a3-4c30-8b02-08923119346a/content

Mahal, A. (2014). Facilitator's and trainer's toolkit: Engage and energize participants for success in meetings, classes, and workshop. Technics Publications.

Mercer, M. (2025). *Oracy: the transformative power of finding your voice*. Bodley Head.

Ofsted. (2024). *Telling the story: The English education subject report*. Available at: https://www.gov.uk/government/publications/subject-report-series-english/telling-the-story-the-english-education-subject-report

Oracy Education Commission. (2024). *We need to talk: The report of the Commission on the future of oracy education in England*. Available at: https://oracyeducationcommission.co.uk/wp-content/uploads/2024/10/Future-of-Oracy-v23-web-13.pdf

Reif, F. (2010). Applying cognitive science to education: Thinking and learning in scientific and other complex domains. MIT Press.

Sherrington, T. and Caviglioli, O. (2020). *Teaching WalkThrus: Five-step guides to instructional coaching*. John Catt Educational.

Sherrington, T. and Stafford, S. (2018). 'Optimising cognitive load: How to adapt your teaching to the limits of working memory'. *MyCollege Research Hub*. Available at: https://my.chartered.college/research-hub/optimising-cognitive-load-how-to-adapt-your-teaching-to-the-limits-of-working-memory/

Shibli, D. and West, R. (2018). 'Cognitive load theory and its application in the classroom'. *Impact*, 2, pp. 18–20.

Sweller, J. (1998). 'Cognitive load during problem solving: Effects on learning'. *Cognitive Science,* 12(2), pp. 257–285.

Sweller, J., Ayres, P., and Kalyuga, S. (2011). *Cognitive load theory.* Springer.

Thompson, S. (2022). *Berger's "An ethic of excellence" in action.* John Catt Educational.

Voice 21. (2026). *Voice 21 Oracy Education.* Available at: https://voice21.org (Accessed: 5 March 2026)

Webster-Stratton, C. (2007). The Incredible Years teacher classroom management program: guidebook/training manual (5-day workshop materials). The Incredible Years Press.

Wilkinson, A. (1965). *Spoken English.* University of Birmingham, School of Education.

Willingham, D. T. (2009). Why don't students like school? A cognitive scientist answers questions about how the mind works and what it means for the classroom. Jossey-Bass.

Willingham, D. T. (2021). *Why don't students like school?* (2nd ed.). Jossey-Bass.